Anonymus

# Return of judicial rents fixed by Sub-Commissions, and Civil Bill Courts

Notified to Irish Land Comission, January 1891

Anonymus

**Return of judicial rents fixed by Sub-Commissions, and Civil Bill Courts**
*Notified to Irish Land Comission, January 1891*

ISBN/EAN: 9783742810342

Manufactured in Europe, USA, Canada, Australia, Japa

Cover: Foto ©Suzi / pixelio.de

Manufactured and distributed by brebook publishing software
(www.brebook.com)

Anonymus

# Return of judicial rents fixed by Sub-Commissions, and Civil Bill Courts

# Irish Land Commission.

The Land Law (Ireland) Act, 1881, 44 & 45 Victoria, ch. 49.

The Land Law (Ireland) Act, 1851, 30 & 31 Victoria, ch. 23.

---

# RETURN

### ACCORDING TO PROVINCES AND COUNTIES

*OF*

# JUDICIAL RENTS

FIXED BY

## CHIEF COMMISSION,

## SUB-COMMISSIONS,

AND

## CIVIL BILL COURTS,

AS NOTIFIED TO THE IRISH LAND COMMISSION DURING THE MONTH OF

JANUARY, 1891,

SPECIFYING DATES AND AMOUNTS RESPECTIVELY OF THE LAST INCREASE
OF RENT WHERE ASCERTAINED;

ALSO

RENTS FIXED UPON THE REPORTS OF VALUERS APPOINTED BY THE IRISH LAND
COMMISSION ON THE JOINT APPLICATIONS OF LANDLORDS AND TENANTS.

---

Presented to both Houses of Parliament by Command of Her Majesty.

---

DUBLIN:

# INDEX.

# SUMMARIES FOR JANUARY, 1891.

Summary showing, according to Provinces and Counties, the Number of Cases in which Judicial Rents have been Fixed by Chief and Sub-Commissions, under the Land Law (Ireland) Act, 1881, during the Month of January, 1891; and also the Acreages, Tenement Valuations, Former Rents, and Judicial Rents of the Holdings.

| Province and County. | Number of Cases in which Judicial Rents have been Fixed. | Acreage. | | | Tenement Valuation. | | | Former Rent. | | | Judicial Rent. | | |
|---|---|---|---|---|---|---|---|---|---|---|---|---|---|
| | | A. | R. | P. | £ | s. | d. | £ | s. | d. | £ | s. | d. |
| ULSTER— | | | | | | | | | | | | | |
| Antrim, | 1 | 52 | 2 | 23 | 80 | 5 | 0 | 150 | 0 | 0 | 100 | 0 | 0 |
| Donegal, | 60 | 1,357 | 0 | 24 | 535 | 17 | 0 | 744 | 13 | 7 | 623 | 5 | 6 |
| Down, | 37 | 516 | 0 | 30 | 752 | 5 | 0 | 678 | 1 | 3 | 547 | 4 | 0 |
| Monaghan, | 2 | 71 | 1 | 23 | 4 | 5 | 0 | 18 | 0 | 0 | 12 | 0 | 0 |
| Tyrone, | 5 | 351 | 1 | 13 | 234 | 10 | 0 | 241 | 16 | 0 | 306 | 0 | 0 |
| Totals, | 103 | 2,691 | 0 | 33 | 1,711 | 2 | 0 | 1,526 | 12 | 9 | 1,500 | 10 | 6 |
| LEINSTER— | | | | | | | | | | | | | |
| Dublin, | 3 | 124 | 3 | 9 | 197 | 15 | 0 | 240 | 0 | 8 | 178 | 0 | 0 |
| Kildare, | 1 | 891 | 3 | 15 | 116 | 0 | 0 | 135 | 15 | 0 | 115 | 0 | 0 |
| Kilkenny, | 3 | 87 | 3 | 11 | 89 | 5 | 0 | 81 | 19 | 10 | 31 | 0 | 0 |
| King's, | 1 | 12 | 0 | 13 | 7 | 5 | 0 | 7 | 10 | 0 | 5 | 0 | 0 |
| Meath, | 1 | 811 | 3 | 34 | 703 | 15 | 0 | 785 | 15 | 0 | 792 | 16 | 0 |
| Queen's, | 20 | 617 | 1 | 23 | 265 | 10 | 0 | 376 | 11 | 5 | 871 | 19 | 0 |
| Wicklow, | 25 | 2,139 | 3 | 4 | 994 | 3 | 0 | 1,165 | 19 | 5 | 945 | 14 | 8 |
| Totals, | 53 | 3,818 | 3 | 33 | 2,385 | 19 | 0 | 2,765 | 3 | 6 | 2,287 | 3 | 5 |
| CONNAUGHT— | | | | | | | | | | | | | |
| Galway, | 16 | 589 | 0 | 34 | 911 | 16 | 0 | 833 | 5 | 6 | 173 | 4 | 0 |
| Leitrim, | 40 | 1,000 | 0 | 2 | 371 | 7 | 0 | 430 | 1 | 5 | 331 | 3 | 0 |
| Roscommon, | 73 | 1,425 | 1 | 7 | 661 | 11 | 0 | 616 | 19 | 11 | 533 | 4 | 0 |
| Totals, | 157 | 3,014 | 2 | 8 | 1,344 | 14 | 0 | 1,185 | 5 | 0 | 1,087 | 11 | 0 |
| MUNSTER— | | | | | | | | | | | | | |
| Clare, | 6 | 133 | 0 | 5 | 31 | 4 | 0 | 56 | 7 | 2 | 46 | 19 | 0 |
| Cork, | 1 | 3 | 3 | 0 | 5 | 14 | 0 | 6 | 0 | 0 | 4 | 0 | 0 |
| Limerick, | 32 | 640 | 0 | 1 | 103 | 0 | 0 | 098 | 18 | 4 | 199 | 19 | 0 |
| Tipperary, | 35 | 1,490 | 0 | 7 | 923 | 17 | 0 | 1,804 | 5 | 1 | 831 | 13 | 10 |
| Totals, | 74 | 2,272 | 3 | 13 | 1,433 | 15 | 0 | 1,954 | 10 | 9 | 1,480 | 10 | 10 |

## IRELAND.

| | | | | | | | | | | | | | |
|---|---|---|---|---|---|---|---|---|---|---|---|---|---|
| ULSTER, | 103 | 2,691 | 2 | 33 | 1,711 | 2 | 0 | 1,526 | 12 | 9 | 1,500 | 10 | 6 |
| LEINSTER, | 53 | 6,818 | 3 | 33 | 2,936 | 13 | 0 | 2,786 | 9 | 6 | 2,287 | 3 | 5 |
| CONNAUGHT, | 157 | 3,014 | 2 | 8 | 1,344 | 14 | 0 | 1,185 | 5 | 0 | 1,087 | 11 | 0 |
| MUNSTER, | 74 | 2,272 | 3 | 13 | 1,433 | 15 | 0 | 1,954 | 10 | 9 | 1,480 | 10 | 10 |
| TOTALS | 882 | 11.797 | 3 | 15 | 8,735 | 4 | 0 | 8,063 | 1 | 5 | 8,658 | 3 | 3 |

NOTE.—For Values' Decisions, see page 84.

# CIVIL BILL COURTS.

## SUMMARY FOR JANUARY, 1891

Cases in which Judicial Rents have been fixed by Civil Bill Courts under the Land Law (Ireland) Act, 1881, and notified to the Irish Land Commission during the Month of January, 1891.

| Province and County. | Number of Cases in which Judicial Rents have been fixed. | Acreage. | | | Tenement Valuation. | | | Former Rent. | | | Judicial Rent. | | |
|---|---|---|---|---|---|---|---|---|---|---|---|---|---|
| | | Statute Acres | | | £ s. d. | | | £ s. d. | | | £ s. d. | | |
| **ULSTER—** | | A. R. P. | | | | | | | | | | | |
| Cavan, | 21 | 331 | 3 | 17 | 168 | 10 | 0 | 192 | 14 | 10 | 148 | 15 | 0 |
| Fermanagh, | 2 | 68 | 3 | 38 | 40 | 0 | 0 | 51 | 7 | 1 | 41 | 2 | 6 |
| Total, | 23 | 400 | 3 | 15 | 229 | 10 | 0 | 244 | 2 | 6 | 188 | 15 | 6 |
| **LEINSTER—** | | | | | | | | | | | | | |
| Kildare, | 2 | 139 | 8 | 11 | 77 | 10 | 0 | 79 | 0 | 0 | 73 | 0 | 0 |
| Kilkenny, | 1 | 57 | 1 | 21 | 67 | 0 | 0 | 68 | 0 | 0 | 56 | 0 | 0 |
| King's, | 1 | 7 | 1 | 7 | 9 | 8 | 0 | 9 | 0 | 0 | 7 | 0 | 0 |
| Meath, | 2 | 228 | 0 | 6 | 177 | 5 | 0 | 182 | 18 | 2 | 150 | 0 | 0 |
| Queen's, | 1 | 38 | 3 | 9 | 33 | 0 | 0 | 22 | 0 | 6 | 17 | 0 | 0 |
| Wicklow, | 3 | 53 | 0 | 7 | 33 | 10 | 0 | 53 | 0 | 0 | 42 | 7 | 0 |
| Total, | 10 | 534 | 1 | 21 | 378 | 10 | 0 | 434 | 16 | 8 | 341 | 7 | 0 |
| **CONNAUGHT—** | | | | | | | | | | | | | |
| Mayo, | 17 | 173 | 0 | 20 | 91 | 0 | 0 | 107 | 15 | 11 | 89 | 18 | 0 |
| **MUNSTER—** | | | | | | | | | | | | | |
| Clare, | 4 | 41 | 0 | 17 | 23 | 8 | 0 | 23 | 5 | 4 | 23 | 8 | 0 |
| Cork, | 2 | 45 | 0 | 0 | 64 | 15 | 0 | 79 | 8 | 8 | 52 | 0 | 6 |
| Tipperary, | 2 | 154 | 1 | 21 | 108 | 15 | 0 | 154 | 17 | 6 | 177 | 10 | 0 |
| Total, | 8 | 205 | 1 | 38 | 196 | 13 | 0 | 265 | 11 | 6 | 210 | 16 | 0 |

IRELAND.

# LEASEHOLDERS.

## SUMMARY FOR JANUARY, 1891.

Summary showing, according to Provinces and Counties, the number of Cases in which Judicial Rents have been fixed by Chief and Sub-Commissions, under the Land Law (Ireland) Act, 1887, during the Month of January, 1891, and also the Acreages, Tenement Valuations, Former Rents, and Judicial Rents of the Holdings.

| Province and County. | Number of Cases in which Judicial Rents have been fixed. | Acreage. | | | Tenement Valuation. | | | Former Rent. | | | Judicial Rent. | | |
|---|---|---|---|---|---|---|---|---|---|---|---|---|---|
| | | A. | R. | P. | £ | s. | d. | £ | s. | d. | £ | s. | d. |
| **Ulster—** | | **Acres** | | | | | | | | | | | |
| Antrim, | 7 | 480 | 3 | 35 | 390 | 10 | 0 | 317 | 19 | 3 | 270 | 13 | 0 |
| Armagh, | 1 | 44 | 1 | 0 | 43 | 10 | 0 | 72 | 7 | 6 | 48 | 0 | 0 |
| Cavan, | 3 | 110 | 3 | 4 | 43 | 1 | 0 | 41 | 7 | 3 | 33 | 7 | 0 |
| Donegal, | 11 | 493 | 3 | 15 | 280 | 0 | 0 | 434 | 3 | 10 | 333 | 16 | 0 |
| Down, | 33 | 600 | 0 | 33 | 343 | 10 | 0 | 496 | 15 | 5 | 339 | 16 | 0 |
| Londonderry, | 4 | 367 | 0 | 17 | 318 | 0 | 0 | 309 | 9 | 0 | 312 | 9 | 0 |
| Monaghan, | 3 | 94 | 2 | 13 | 97 | 0 | 0 | 44 | 3 | 8 | 56 | 0 | 0 |
| Tyrone, | 15 | 411 | 0 | 30 | 318 | 0 | 0 | 323 | 6 | 6½ | 387 | 3 | 2½ |
| **Totals,** | **65** | **2,584** | **1** | **39** | **1,864** | **13** | **0** | **2,174** | **14** | **4½** | **1,660** | **4** | **2½** |
| **Leinster—** | | | | | | | | | | | | | |
| Carlow, | 5 | 325 | 3 | 31 | 198 | 3 | 0 | 239 | 8 | 1 | 149 | 0 | 0 |
| Dublin, | 10 | 633 | 1 | 30 | 781 | 5 | 0 | 1,079 | 16 | 4 | 789 | 19 | 4 |
| Kildare, | 3 | 161 | 3 | 34 | 104 | 10 | 0 | 133 | 0 | 0 | 113 | 0 | 0 |
| Kilkenny, | 3 | 271 | 3 | 0 | 116 | 8 | 0 | 170 | 0 | 0 | 130 | 0 | 0 |
| King's, | 3 | 139 | 0 | 25 | 87 | 15 | 0 | 73 | 0 | 0 | 63 | 0 | 0 |
| Longford, | 3 | 70 | 2 | 38 | 43 | 0 | 0 | 71 | 0 | 0 | 40 | 0 | 0 |
| Louth, | 1 | 30 | 0 | 34 | 33 | 0 | 0 | 41 | 0 | 0 | 34 | 0 | 0 |
| Meath, | 4 | 833 | 3 | 30 | 349 | 10 | 0 | 393 | 10 | 6 | 312 | 15 | 0 |
| Queen's, | 11 | 1,209 | 1 | 1 | 804 | 14 | 6 | 1,335 | 10 | 11 | 855 | 15 | 0 |
| Westmeath, | 3 | 301 | 3 | 31 | 232 | 10 | 0 | 228 | 0 | 11 | 231 | 10 | 0 |
| Wexford, | 1 | 10 | 1 | 20 | 6 | 8 | 0 | 7 | 13 | 4 | 6 | 0 | 0 |
| Wicklow, | 3 | 371 | 3 | 6 | 115 | 16 | 0 | 216 | 10 | 0 | 138 | 0 | 0 |
| **Totals,** | **48** | **4,041** | **2** | **10** | **2,851** | **18** | **0** | **3,838** | **3** | **9½** | **2,915** | **11** | **8** |
| **Connaught—** | | | | | | | | | | | | | |
| Leitrim, | 17 | 493 | 3 | 3 | 314 | 5 | 0 | 360 | 16 | 11 | 293 | 13 | 0 |
| Roscommon, | 3 | 417 | 1 | 53 | 304 | 10 | 0 | 343 | 8 | 7 | 390 | 0 | 0 |
| Sligo, | 1 | 33 | 3 | 30 | 9 | 0 | 0 | 15 | 0 | 5 | 10 | 0 | 0 |
| **Totals,** | **20** | **943** | **2** | **33** | **629** | **15** | **0** | **619** | **5** | **2½** | **693** | **13** | **0** |
| **Munster—** | | | | | | | | | | | | | |
| Clare, | 3 | 479 | 3 | 33 | 94 | 10 | 0 | 137 | 13 | 10 | 97 | 8 | 0 |
| Cork, | 6 | 183 | 1 | 8 | 108 | 19 | 0 | 116 | 14 | 4 | 133 | 10 | 0 |
| Kerry, | 3 | 131 | 3 | 37 | 68 | 0 | 0 | 93 | 14 | 3 | 63 | 0 | 0 |
| Limerick, | 37 | 1,010 | 1 | 89 | 611 | 8 | 6 | 963 | 19 | 7 | 644 | 9 | 8 |
| Tipperary, | 63 | 6,807 | 3 | 19 | 2,633 | 5 | 0 | 2,431 | 9 | 9½ | 2,326 | 3 | 8 |
| Waterford, | 1 | 31 | 3 | 17 | — | | | 43 | 19 | 6 | 31 | 8 | 3 |
| **Totals,** | **99** | **5,797** | **3** | **19** | **3,464** | **10** | **0** | **4,836** | **3** | **2½** | **3,567** | **16** | **1** |

IRELAND.

# CIVIL BILL COURTS.

## LEASEHOLDERS.

### SUMMARY FOR JANUARY, 1891.

Cases in which Judicial Rents have been fixed by the Civil Bill Courts, under the Land Law (Ireland) Act, 1887, and notified to the Irish Land Commission during the Month of January, 1891.

| Province and County. | Number of Cases in which Judicial Rents have been fixed. | Acreage. | | | Former Valuation. | | | Former Rent. | | | Judicial Rent. | | |
|---|---|---|---|---|---|---|---|---|---|---|---|---|---|
| | | Statute Acres. | | | £ s. d. | | | £ s. d. | | | £ s. d. | | |
| | | a. r. p. | | | | | | | | | | | |
| ULSTER— | | | | | | | | | | | | | |
| Fermanagh, ... | 3 | 45 | 0 | 12 | 26 | 1 | 0 | 24 | 8 | 8 | 16 | 16 | 0 |
| LEINSTER— | | | | | | | | | | | | | |
| Meath, ... | 7 | 651 | 1 | 29 | 678 | 15 | 0 | 762 | 2 | 10 | 584 | 5 | 0 |
| Wicklow, ... | 1 | 26 | 0 | 3 | 15 | 0 | 0 | 27 | 0 | 0 | 20 | 0 | 0 |
| Totals, ... | 8 | 677 | 1 | 32 | 643 | 15 | 0 | 789 | 2 | 10 | 604 | 5 | 0 |
| CONNAUGHT— | | | | | | | | | | | | | |
| Mayo, ... | 1 | 13 | 0 | 9 | 6 | 0 | 0 | 14 | 0 | 0 | 6 | 10 | 0 |
| MUNSTER— | | | | | | | | | | | | | |
| Cork, ... | 2 | 196 | 1 | 35 | 148 | 0 | 0 | 163 | 4 | 8 | 127 | 10 | 0 |
| Tipperary, ... | 2 | 68 | 2 | 23 | 51 | 3 | 0 | 55 | 15 | 0 | 43 | 5 | 0 |
| Totals, ... | 4 | 235 | 0 | 20 | 200 | 5 | 0 | 218 | 19 | 8 | 170 | 15 | 0 |

## IRELAND.

| | | | | | | | | | | | | | |
|---|---|---|---|---|---|---|---|---|---|---|---|---|---|
| ULSTER, — | 3 | 45 | 0 | 12 | 26 | 5 | 0 | 24 | 8 | 8 | 16 | 16 | 0 |
| LEINSTER, — | 8 | 677 | 1 | 32 | 643 | 15 | 0 | 789 | 2 | 10 | 604 | 5 | 0 |
| CONNAUGHT, — | 1 | 13 | 0 | 9 | 6 | 0 | 0 | 14 | 0 | 0 | 6 | 10 | 0 |
| MUNSTER, — | 4 | 235 | 0 | 20 | 200 | 5 | 0 | 218 | 19 | 8 | 170 | 15 | 0 |
| TOTALS, — | 15 | 1,017 | 2 | 23 | 876 | 5 | 0 | 1,075 | 10 | 9 | 802 | 6 | 0 |

# PROVINCE OF

## COUNTY OF

| Names of Assistant Commissioners by whom Cases were decided. | No. | Name of Tenant. | Name of Landlord. | Townland. |
|---|---|---|---|---|
| Assistant Commissioners— <br> F. Gahan (Legal). <br> J. M. Weir. <br> L. W. Byrne. | 4078 | Richard M. Douglas, ... | Sampson Allen ... ... | Newtownboy, — |

## COUNTY OF

| Assistant Commissioners— <br> D. Tighe (Legal). <br> R. B. Blackwood. <br> R. O'Kelly. | No. | | | |
|---|---|---|---|---|
| | 5229 | John Henderson, ... | Earl of Erne, ... ... | Ballinahrina, ... |
| | 5230 | James Gallagher, — | James Watt, ... ... | Kirkcassidy, — |
| | 5231 | James Mulhern, ... | Robert Laskey, ... ... | Drummeera, ... |
| | 5232 | James MacDermott, — | Viscountess Southwell and others, Trustees of Lord Southwell, a minor. | Glenamer, ... |
| | 5233 | Cornelius McMonagle, | do. ... ... | do. ... |
| | 5234 | John McMonagle, ... | Alexander J. R. Stewart, ... | Carraghlena, ... |
| | 5235 | Anne Boulston, ... | do. ... ... | Edenlarroon, ... |
| | 5236 | William Montgomery, | Samuel Saunderson, ... | Master Cunningham, |
| | 5237 | Do, ... — | do. ... | do. — |
| | 5238 | John Hunter, ... | do. ... — | do. ... |
| | 5239 | William Galbraith, ... | Charles M. Calhoun, ... | Carrickballyloory and another. |
| | 5240 | Ellen Gallagher, — | Sir Samuel H. Hayes, Bart., | Dresballagh, ... |
| | 5241 | Michael McGinley, — | do. ... — | Ratherlog, ... |
| | 5242 | Hannah Cromblih, — | John R. Boyd, ... — | Killymassny, ... |
| | 5243 | James Carbeery, ... | do. — ... | do. ... |
| | 5244 | James Bradley, ... | do. ... ... | Ballymaseul, ... |
| | 5245 | James Park, ... | do. ... — | do. ... |
| | 5246 | George McKinney, ... | do. ... — | Ardshee ... |

# ULSTER.

## ANTRIM.

| Extent of Holding, Statute. | Poor Law Valuation | Former Rent. | Judicial Rent. | Observations. | Value of Tenancy. |
|---|---|---|---|---|---|
| a. r. p. | £ s. d. | £ s. d. | £ s. d. | | £ s. d. |
| 69 2 32 | 50 5 0 | 150 0 0 | 100 0 0 | | |

## DONEGAL.

| | | | | | |
|---|---|---|---|---|---|
| 77 0 9 | 24 10 0 | 33 11 0 | 77 0 0 | | |
| 33 0 0 | 8 0 0 | 7 6 0 | 8 7 6 | | |
| 6 3 13 | 4 0 0 | 4 0 0 | 4 6 6 | With ¼ grazing of 16£s. 3s. 10½. and turbary thereon. | |
| 11 0 0 | 4 3 0 | 6 9 6 | 4 17 6 | | |
| 8 0 0 | 4 5 0 | 1 18 0 | 3 15 0 | | |
| 61 0 0 | 9 10 0 | 10 7 0 | 7 10 0 | | |
| 31 0 30 | 20 13 0 | 15 0 0 | 13 0 0 | | |
| 5 3 12 | 5 0 0 | 6 0 0 | 6 0 0 | | |
| 10 3 8 | 6 0 0 | 8 0 0 | 8 0 0 | | |
| 10 3 30 | 9 16 0 | 8 8 0 | 7 7 6 | | |
| 54 0 37 | 38 5 0 | 85 7 0 | 30 0 0 | | |
| 13 0 37 | 8 5 0 | 3 0 0 | 3 8 0 | | |
| 41 3 30 | 16 13 0 | 15 8 0 | 15 6 0 | | |
| 5 0 16 | 3 6 0 | 4 0 0 | 3 0 0 | | |
| 18 3 17 | 6 10 0 | 6 6 0 | 4 15 0 | | |
| 16 3 30 | 10 5 0 | 11 0 0 | 8 10 0 | | |
| 34 1 23 | 9 13 0 | 11 15 0 | 8 17 6 | | |
| 66 1 10 | 41 0 0 | 35 0 0 | 32 0 0 | | |
| 4 3 34 | 8 10 0 | 8 19 3 | 3 13 6 | | |
| 63 1 30 | 53 5 0 | 53 12 0 | 45 6 0 | | |

| Names of Assistant Commissioners by whom Cases were decided. | No. | Name of Tenant. | Name of Landlord. | Townland. |
|---|---|---|---|---|
| **Assistant Commissioners—** | | | | |
| D. TOOMEY (Legal). R. B. HEMPTON. E. O'HALL. | 6349 | Henry McOniscum, Liectd. Admx. of Arthur McOniscum. | Marquis of Londonderry, ... | Ballydavra, — |
| | 6350 | Samuel McKinley, — | do. ... ... | do. ... |
| | 6351 | Robert Platt, — | do. ... — | Drain, — |
| | 6352 | John McKinley, ... | do. ... — | Vaugh, — |
| D. TOOMEY (Legal). O. VANDELEUR. H. JOHNSTON. | 6353 | T. R. Henry, ... | Colonel J. H. T. Thornton, mentioned in name of Captain J. H. R. T. Thornton. | Magherowodie, — |
| | 6354 | Mathew McHale, — | Mary A. O'Daugherty & ors., | Killygordon, — |
| | 6355 | Thomas A. Holmes, ... | Rev. Richard T. Ogden, ... | Raphoe, — |
| | 6356 | Jane Kilgrena, Liecd. Admx. of Robert Kilgrena. | Irish Land Commission v. Bryce, | Alt, Upper, — |
| | 6357 | Donald McCrudden, — | Lady Darcus J. F. Chichester, | Donish, — |
| | 6358 | Francis Elliot, ... | Colonel R. G. Montgomery, ... | Tullydonnell, — |
| | 6359 | Galbraith Thompson, ... | do. — | Ourvey, — |
| | 6360 | Rev. Robert Buchan, — | do. — | Ourvey, Town Parks. |
| | 6361 | James Toy, — | Captain A. M. Stewart, | Munterbeeny, ... |
| | 6362 | Samuel Eaton, ... | do. — | do. ... |
| | 6363 | William Lynch, — | do. — | do. ... |
| | 6364 | Patrick Lynch, Liecd. Admx. of Martin Lynch. | do. ... — | do. ... |
| | 6365 | Catherine M. Eaton, ... | do. — | do. — |
| | 6366 | Joseph Laird, ... | do. — | do. — |
| | 6367 | William Eaton, ... | do. — | do. — |
| | 6368 | Do., ... | do. ... — | do. — |
| | 6369 | John Eaton, ... | do. — | do. — |
| | 6370 | Samuel Eaton, — | do. — | do. — |
| | 6371 | Joseph Laird, ... | do. ... — | do. — |
| | 6372 | James Eaton, ... | do. — | do. — |
| | 6373 | William Barnett, — | do. — | do. — |
| | 6374 | Mary Maxwell, — | do. — | Coolederry, ... |
| | 6375 | Patrick McOranaghan, jr. | do. — | do. — |
| | 6376 | Thomas A. Holmes, ... | do. — | do. — |

## DONEGAL—continued

| Extent of Holding. Acres. | Poor Law Valuation. | Former Rent. | Present Rent. | |
|---|---|---|---|---|
| A. R. P. | £ s. d. | £ s. d. | £ s. d. | |
| 17 0 16 | 11 10 0 | 6 16 9 | 7 8 0 | |
| 31 5 16 | 24 10 0 | 23 12 4 | 20 0 0 | |
| 84 3 14 | 18 0 0 | 17 6 6 | 17 6 8 | |
| 62 1 7 | 44 5 0 | 40 0 0 | 34 10 0 | |
| | | | | |
| | | | | |
| | | | | |
| 26 2 0 | uncertained | 22 1 10 | 19 0 0 | |
| 8 2 0 | 11 0 0 | 20 0 0 | 18 0 0 | |
| 5 0 10 | 6 10 0 | 10 10 0 | 7 7 0 | |
| 6 0 6 | 6 10 0 | 4 19 10 | 4 6 0 | |
| 13 0 0 | 3 10 0 | 6 3 3 | 2 11 0 | |
| 34 2 31 | uncertained | 23 6 3 | 17 0 0 | |
| 16 6 6 | 22 6 0 | 20 16 11 | 17 6 0 | |
| 13 6 8 | uncertained | 18 19 0 | 14 0 0 | |
| 26 0 62 | 16 14 0 | 13 3 16 | 10 16 0 | |
| 57 0 6 | 16 17 0 | 18 16 3 | 6 5 0 | |
| 17 5 60 | 9 15 0 | 8 16 7 | 9 0 0 | |
| 23 8 16 | 3 15 0 | 6 17 3 | 6 16 0 | |
| 31 1 0 | 7 0 0 | 7 12 8 | 6 10 0 | |
| 16 3 24 | uncertained | 6 16 21 | 8 10 0 | |
| 18 8 2 | 6 1 0 | 3 8 6 | 2 19 6 | |
| 2 3 70 | 1 10 6 | 8 6 0 | 1 12 0 | |
| 19 6 67 | 2 10 6 | 3 6 6 | 2 11 0 | |
| 18 3 16 | 3 16 6 | 4 16 6 | 4 6 6 | |
| 18 0 16 | uncertained | 2 10 0 | 3 16 0 | |
| 27 6 6 | 12 6 6 | 13 16 8 | 10 10 0 | |
| 48 0 16 | 6 0 6 | 6 6 0 | 6 10 0 | |
| 16 0 86 | 2 10 0 | 10 6 6 | 7 16 0 | |
| 4 1 16 | 6 10 6 | 6 10 0 | 8 6 0 | |
| 19 1 14 | 16 19 6 | 30 0 6 | 16 6 0 | |

COUNTY OF

| Name of Assistant Commissioner by whom Court was decided. | No. | Name of Tenant. | Name of Landlord. | Townland. |
|---|---|---|---|---|
| Assistant Commissioner—<br>D. TOUHY (Legal).<br>H. DOLAN.<br>E. DUNLAP. | 6177 | John Graham, | Mary C. E. Johnston, | Tullynaprain, |
| | 6178 | Nixon Graham, | do. | do. |
| | 6179 | Paddy Kennedy, | H. G. M. Stewart, | Newtown Drin-gotitah. |
| | 6180 | Edward Wilson, | do. | Drumard, |
| | 6181 | James O'Donnell, | Henry Brown & anor., Trustees of Thomas Connolly. | Gaughy, |
| | 6182 | Mary Anne Kelly, | do. | Mullinmela, |
| | 6183 | Bridget O'Donnell, | do. | Legboy. |
| | 6184 | William Travers, | do. | Ormullis, |
| | 6185 | Catherine Kirkpatrick, | do. | Tullywon, |
| | 6186 | Patrick Martin, | do. | Mullinmela |
| | 6187 | Mary McFhelim & anor., | do. | Rossilly. |
| | 6188 | Charles Gorman, | do. | Oraughn, |
| | | | | Total, — |

COUNTY OF

| Assistant Commissioners—<br>R. GREER (Legal).<br>H. GARLAND.<br>H. CRAWFORD. | 6302 | William Finley, | R. H. Kerr, | Knockbracken, |
|---|---|---|---|---|
| | 6303 | John Finlay, | do. | do. |
| | 6304 | Francis Sheppard, | James C. Price, | Glassdrumacaad, |
| | 6305 | Hugh McVey, | do. | Lisdalgin, |
| | 6306 | James Shaw, | do. | Corrlakmeeaaaa, |
| | 6307 | George McCready, | Viscount Bridport and anor., Trustees of Marquis of Downshire. | Edentrillick, |
| | 6308 | John Hamilton, Esqr. of William Hack, | Omar C. Nelson and another, Trustees of H. Nelson. | Lappagas, |
| | 6309 | Rachel Boston and anor., Extrx. of Thomas Boston. | Robert Waddell, | Drumra & another, |
| | 6310 | Thomas Gardiner, | do. | Maralin, |
| | 6311 | Joseph Kee and another, Exors. of Samuel O'Dumple, deceased. | John Mulholland Trustee of B. W. B. Kee. | Ballykine, |
| | 6312 | William McKelvey, | do. | Glassdrumaaad, |
| | 6313 | Thomas McNeill, | do. | do. |
| | 6314 | Joseph Donvnndy, | do. | do. |

## DONEGAL—*continued.*

| Extent of Holding. Statute. | Poor Law Valuation. | Former Rent. | Judicial Rent. | Observations. |
|---|---|---|---|---|
| A. R. P. | £ s. d. | £ s. d. | £ s. d. | |
| 62 3 6 | 24 0 0 | 23 6 6 | 19 13 0 | |
| 63 2 33 | 15 16 0 | 19 1 4 | 14 16 0 | |
| 31 3 70 | 7 10 0 | 7 2 0 | 6 0 0 | |
| 14 0 30 | 5 10 0 | 6 0 0 | 4 0 0 | |
| 7 2 30 | unascertained, | 4 5 0 | 4 0 0 | |
| 17 1 0 | 5 5 0 | 6 0 0 | 5 10 0 | |
| 16 0 37 | unascertained, | 7 0 0 | 5 0 0 | |
| 22 2 15 | do. | 4 2 4 | 4 2 4 | |
| 54 0 15 | 21 10 0 | 18 6 8 | 18 4 6 | |
| 14 0 31 | 4 10 0 | 5 1 0 | 4 6 0 | |
| 22 0 10 | 10 6 0 | 9 10 0 | 9 0 0 | |
| 45 3 18 | 8 0 0 | 8 8 0 | 7 13 0 | |
| 1,357 0 31 | 853 17 0 | 714 13 7 | 630 8 9 | |

DOWN.

COUNTY OF

| Name of Assistant Commissioners by whom Cases were decided. | No. | Name of Tenant. | Name of Landlord. | Townland. |
|---|---|---|---|---|
| Assistant Commissioners— | | | | |
| E. Gwynn (Legal). | 6315 | Samuel Martin, | ... | John Mulholland, Trustee of R. W. A Ker. | Ballykine, | ... |
| E. (Ireland). | 6316 | George Halliday, | ... | do. | ... | do. | ... |
| S. Crawford. | 6317 | Samuel Martin, | ... | do. | ... | Ballywrown, | ... |
| | 6318 | David Ker Maitland, | ... | do. | ... | do. | ... |
| | 6319 | John Rea, ... | ... | do. | ... | do. | ... |
| | 6320 | Joseph Somerville, | ... | do. | ... | do. | ... |
| | 6321 | John Bell, ... | ... | do. | ... | do. | ... |
| | 6322 | Do. ... | ... | do. | ... | do. | ... |
| | 6323 | William Smyth, | ... | do. | ... | Magheralruach, | |
| | 6324 | David Blakeley, | ... | do. | ... | Crowrytownad, | ... |
| | 6325 | William Priestley, | ... | do. | ... | Clantmagunland, | |
| | 6326 | John M.Keown, | ... | do. | ... | Barroch, | ... |
| | 6327 | James Smith, | ... | do. | ... | Ballykine | ... |
| | 6328 | Martin Campbell, | ... | do. | ... | Cargyrawy, | ... |
| | 6329 | Thomas Gilmore, | ... | do. | ... | Clantmagunland, | |
| | 6330 | Francis King, | ... | do. | ... | Barton, | ... |
| | 6331 | Thomas Gilmore, | ... | do. | ... | do. | ... |
| | 6332 | Jacob Morrison, | ... | George T. Hunter, | ... | Cargyrawy, | ... |
| | 6333 | John Keeblin, | ... | do. | ... | do. | ... |
| | 6334 | John Prden, | ... | Thomas Brown, ... | Tullymire, | |
| | 6335 | David Hammill, | ... | do. | ... | do. | ... |
| | 6336 | Henry Conboy, | ... | Hastings Dent, ... | Banoge, | ... |
| | 6337 | Do. ... | ... | do. | ... | do. | ... |
| | 6338 | Andrew Stevenson, | ... | Robert P. Harding, Assignee of R. K. Boyd, | Monlough, | |
| | | | | Total, | ... |

COUNTY OF

## DOWN—continued.

| Extent of Holding. Statute. | Poor Law Valuation. | Former Rent. | Judicial Rent. | Observations. |
|---|---|---|---|---|
| A. R. P. | £ s. d. | £ s. d. | £ s. d. | |
| 18 0 15 | 12 5 0 | 13 0 0 | 12 0 0 | |
| 3 5 0 | 7 5 0 | 6 12 0 | 6 0 0 | |
| 34 1 6 | 17 10 0 | 13 1 0 | 13 5 0 | |
| 58 2 30 | 37 10 0 | 37 0 0 | 20 0 0 | |
| 43 3 10 | 30 10 0 | 19 6 0 | 14 5 0 | |
| 14 1 0 | 12 6 0 | 10 10 0 | 9 15 0 | |
| 8 3 35 | 7 10 0 | 7 11 0 | 6 0 0 | |
| 4 5 20 | 4 0 0 | 4 4 0 | 3 15 0 | |
| 14 1 30 | 9 0 0 | 6 11 0 | 6 0 0 | |
| 48 1 30 | 51 10 0 | 45 0 0 | 38 10 0 | Provision has been made in this case as regards a labourer. |
| 14 3 0 | 11 5 0 | 9 10 0 | 9 0 0 | |
| 13 3 30 | 9 10 0 | 10 0 0 | 7 0 0 | |
| 11 1 16 | 8 5 0 | 8 7 0 | 7 10 0 | |
| 13 1 0 | 12 5 0 | 11 0 0 | 9 5 0 | |
| 18 0 35 | 16 0 0 | 14 8 0 | 10 15 0 | |
| 33 3 0 | 16 5 0 | 12 1 0 | 10 15 0 | |
| 80 3 15 | 30 0 0 | 24 1 0 | 18 0 0 | |
| 31 1 35 | 27 10 0 | 25 0 0 | 20 0 0 | Rent changed in 1882 £ s. d. from . . 31 0 0 do. 9 10 0 |
| 7 3 30 | 5 0 0 | 7 1 0 | 3 10 0 | |
| 1 1 35 | no government. | 1 10 0 | 1 10 0 | |
| 183 3 1 | 343 0 0 | 308 0 0 | 143 0 0 | |
| 7 3 4 | 7 10 0 | 9 8 3 | 7 0 0 | |
| 5 0 0 | 6 5 0 | 5 3 0 | 5 0 0 | |
| 5 0 15 | 6 5 0 | 5 18 3 | 4 10 0 | |
| 878 0 33 | 783 5 0 | 675 1 3 | 557 4 0 | |

MONAGHAN.

| Name of Assistant Commissioners by whom Cases were decided. | No. | Name of Tenant. | Name of Landlord. |
|---|---|---|---|
| Head Commission: | 7617 | Hugh Sampson, | — | Mrs. A. C. Maxw. |
| | | | |
| Assistant Commissioners— | 7518 | David McDonald, | ... | Caroline Hamilton. |
| D. Twomey (Legal). | 7519 | John Kee, continued in name of Jane Kee. | George Marks, | ... |
| R. M. Hartford. | 7520 | Edward Browne, | — | J. F. Bennell, | ... |
| K. O'Kelly. | 7521 | Mary A. Gamble, | — | Duke of Abercorn, |
| | 7522 | Do., | ... | — | do. | — |
| | 7523 | Do., | — | ... | do. | ... |
| | 7524 | Thomas Browne, | | do. | ... |

| | | | | | | |
|---|---|---|---|---|---|---|
| 11 | 0 | 0 | ...cart.ined, | | | |
| 31 | 0 | 0 | 24 | 0 | 0 | |
| 6 | 1 | 11 | 6 | 8 | 0 | |
| 73 | 0 | 16 | 8 | 10 | 0 | |
| 147 | 1 | 6 | 100 | 10 | 0 | |
| 14 | 0 | 30 | 14 | 0 | 0 | |
| 43 | 0 | 0 | 43 | 15 | 0 | |
| 331 | 1 | 13 | 235 | 10 | 0 | |

# LEINSTER.

## DUBLIN.

| Names of Assistant Commissioners by whom Cases were decided. | No. | Name of Tenant. | Name of Landlord. |
|---|---|---|---|
| Assistant Commissioners— |  |  |  |
| L. Doyle (Legal), J. M. Carmela. E. O. Peel. | 2180 | Michael Kennedy, sued in name of Joseph Walsh. | W. H. Green, |
|  | 2181 | Thomas Kelly, ... | Mrs. Emma E. Clifton |

| Assistant Commissioners— |  |  |  |
|---|---|---|---|
| M. T. Cogan (Legal), W. G. Orpen. J. Rice. | 1872 | Richard Hooley, ... | Captain Patrickson, |

# TABLE OF JUDICIAL RENTS.

## KILKENNY.

| Extent of Holding. Statute. | Poor Law Valuation. | Former Rent. | Judicial Rent. | Observations. |
|---|---|---|---|---|
| A. R. P. | £ s. d. | £ s. d. | £ s. d. | |
| 77 2 36 | 23 0 0 | 20 9 10 | 15 0 0 | By consent. |
| 10 0 15 | 10 5 0 | 31 10 0 | 13 0 0 | do. |
| 91 3 11 | 33 5 0 | 51 19 10 | 24 0 0 | |

## COUNTY.

| | | | | |
|---|---|---|---|---|
| 12 0 03 | 7 5 0 | 7 10 0 | 6 0 0 | By consent. |

## MEATH.

| | | | | |
|---|---|---|---|---|
| 611 3 24 | 703 15 0 | 765 13 0 | 762 16 0 | The rent in this case was fixed by consent of the parties at the sitting of the Court in Dublin. |

## COUNTY.

| | | | | |
|---|---|---|---|---|
| 16 0 31 | 12 8 0 | 13 15 6 | 8 0 0 | |
| 47 1 2 | 16 10 0 | 30 6 0 | 18 10 0 | Rent changed in 1847 from £ s. d. 37 0 0 |
| 68 1 10 | 23 10 0 | 36 15 6 | 35 0 0 | 1856, 62 15 3 |
| 82 0 33 | 38 0 6 | 63 0 0 | 42 0 0 | |
| 30 0 0 | 13 5 0 | 16 1 10 | 13 0 0 | |
| 6 0 13 | 4 0 0 | 5 0 0 | 3 10 0 | |
| 7 0 7 | 3 10 0 | 8 10 0 | 4 10 0 | |
| 62 3 10 | 21 15 0 | 26 0 0 | 20 0 0 | |
| 21 0 14 | 10 10 0 | 16 18 4 | 8 10 0 | |
| 139 1 21 | 45 10 0 | 60 0 0 | 30 0 0 | 1876, 60 0 0 |
| 4 3 31 | 4 0 0 | 5 0 0 | 6 0 0 | |

| Names at Assistant Commissioners by whom Cases were decided. | No. | Name of Tenant. | Name of Landlord. | Townland. |
|---|---|---|---|---|
| Assistant Commissioners— | | | | |
| W. S. HOYTE | 1684 | Ellen Keegan, | Richard Warburton, | Rathkeash, |
| H. MARTIN. | 1685 | Daniel Dunne, | do. | Rathmiles, |
| | 1686 | William Terrett, | do. | Tynch-gour, |
| | 1687 | Edward Carroll, | do. | Huntington, |
| | 1688 | Denis Dunne, | do. | Rathmiles, |
| | 1689 | John Maher, | do. | Tishogar, |
| | 1690 | Bridget Kavanagh, | do. | Rathmiles, |
| | 1691 | John Grady, | do. | Tisbogar, |
| | 1692 | Bridget Kavanagh, | do. | Rathkeash, |
| | | | | Total, |

COUNTY OF

| HEAD COMMISSION. | 1062 | William Murphy, | Earl of Wicklow, | Knockhouse, |
|---|---|---|---|---|
| Assistant Commissioners— | | | | |
| R. R. LANE (Legal). | 1063 | James Darker, | Marquis of Waterford, | Burgess More, |
| W. G. DE LA POER. | 1064 | Do., | do. | do. |
| J. HAWKESWORTH. | 1065 | Mathew Halpin, | Thomas B. Brown, | Croughan, |
| | 1066 | Do., | do. | do. |
| | 1067 | Edward Commins, | do. | Carrig, |
| | 1068 | Ellen Carroll, | Elizabeth G. Smith, a minor, by J. J. D. Le Touche, her Guardian. | Loskan, |
| | 1069 | Benjamin Butler, | do. | Ballyteaye, |
| | 1060 | James Carroll, | do. | Loskan, |
| | 1061 | Ellen Carroll, | do. | do. |
| | 1062 | Esther Murphy, | Viscount Bridport and anor., Trustees of Marquis of Downshire. | Ballynaslion, |
| | 1063 | Do., | do. | Old Court, |
| | 1064 | James Walsh, | do. | Ballynaslion, |
| | 1065 | Patrick Mullally, | do. | do. |
| | 1066 | Myles Murphy, | do. | Ballynaslion, Upr. |

## COUNTY—*continued.*

| Extent of Holding | Poor Law Valuation. | Former Rent. | Judicial Rent. | Observations. | Value of Tenancy. |
|---|---|---|---|---|---|
| A. R. P. | £ s. d. | £ s. d. | £ s. d. | | £ s. d. |
| 18 2 0 | 8 10 0 | 16 8 1 | 10 10 0 | | |
| 11 0 23 | 8 8 0 | 8 2 0 | 7 0 0 | | |
| 12 5 9 | 10 0 6 | 11 15 0 | 7 10 0 | | |
| 4 1 0 | 3 10 0 | 3 18 10 | 3 16 0 | | |
| 8 8 82 | 7 5 0 | 7 15 2 | 6 0 0 | | |
| 48 1 34 | 30 0 0 | 32 0 0 | 32 6 0 | | |
| 13 0 28 | 5 15 0 | 5 4 0 | 6 4 0 | | |
| 8 1 21 | 5 15 0 | 7 0 0 | 6 0 0 | | |
| 12 3 35 | 8 15 0 | 12 0 0 | 9 0 0 | | |
| 617 1 29 | 284 10 0 | 276 11 8 | 371 19 0 | | |

## WICKLOW.

| | | | | | |
|---|---|---|---|---|---|
| 70 3 34 | 50 0 0 | 48 0 0 | 32 0 0 | The rent in this case was fixed by consent of the parties at the sitting of the Court in Dublin. | |
| 64 0 8 | 63 10 0 | 49 7 6 | 54 0 0 | | |
| 55 3 23 | 53 10 0 | 49 8 8 | 48 9 8 | | |
| 44 7 5 | 38 50 0 | 50 0 0 | 18 0 0 | | |
| 80 1 23 | 7 0 0 | 7 0 0 | 6 15 0 | | |
| 63 3 95 | 81 5 0 | 40 0 0 | 36 0 0 | | |
| 314 0 21 | 14 15 0 | 10 0 0 | 13 0 0 | | |
| 5 0 11 | 6 10 0 | 5 0 0 | 4 10 0 | | |
| 38 0 10 | uncertained | 8 0 0 | 6 10 0 | | |
| 63 1 14 | 5 15 0 | 4 10 0 | 4 10 0 | | |
| 108 3 35 | 17 0 0 | 19 0 0 | 14 0 0 | | |
| 45 1 20 | 21 10 0 | 25 0 0 | 20 0 0 | | |
| 53 6 33 | 17 15 0 | 16 0 0 | 13 10 0 | | |
| 01 1 23 | 19 0 0 | 25 0 0 | 20 0 0 | | |
| 77 0 0 | 15 10 0 | 17 0 0 | 18 10 0 | | |
| 90 3 11 | 44 0 0 | 70 0 0 | 50 0 0 | | |
| 23 1 4 | 59 10 0 | 50 0 0 | 65 0 0 | | |

COUNTY OF

| Name of Assistant Commissioners by whom Cases were decided. | No. | Name of Tenant. | Name of Landlord. | Townland. |
|---|---|---|---|---|
| Assistant Commissioners— R. R. Kane (Legal). W. G. De la Poer. J. Hawksworth. | 1069 | George Phibbs, ... | Viscount Bridport and anr., Trustees of Marquis of Devonshire. | Lurgague, Little, |
| | 1070 | Thomas Richardson, ... | do. ... ... | do. |
| | 1071 | Myles Murphy, ... | do. ... | Ballydonnell, Nth. |
| | 1072 | Luke Murphy, ... | do. ... | Ballynasimon, |
| | 1073 | John Boothman, continued in name of James Boothman. | do. ... | Cnocaunbwrboy. |
| | 1074 | Frank Healy, ... | do. ... | Ballymacallage, |
| | 1075 | John J. Horridge, continued in name of Margaret Major J. Finnимor. | Earl of Milltown, ... | Cloghbine and another. |
| | 1076 | Do., ... | Joseph P. Tynte, ... | Burgage, |
| | | | | Total, |

PROVINCE OF

WICKLOW—*continued.*

| Extent of Holding. Acres. | Poor Law Valuation. | Former Rent. | Judicial Rent. | Observations. | Value at Tenancy. |
|---|---|---|---|---|---|
| A. R. P. | £ s. d. | £ s. d. | £ s. d. | | £ s. d. |
| 41 1 8 | 16 10 0 | 20 0 0 | 14 10 0 | Right to graze on 33a. 3r. Ein of Blackamore Mountain. | |
| 15 0 23 | unascertained. | 6 0 0 | 4 0 0 | Right to graze on ascertained part of Lugnaquo Mountain with 8 others. | |
| 79 3 4 | 16 15 0 | 15 0 0 | 10 10 0 | Right to graze with 4 others on Mountain of Ballylowd, North and South, containing 1542a. 3r. 25p. | |
| 80 1 18 | 15 10 0 | 17 0 0 | 14 0 0 | | |
| 144 0 33 | 130 8 0 | 170 0 0 | 130 0 0 | | |
| 254 1 10 | 45 0 0 | 46 0 0 | 45 0 0 | | |
| 277 0 31 | 163 7 0 | 202 0 0 | 170 0 0 | | |
| 160 0 0 | 113 15 0 | 186 15 4 | 163 0 0 | | |
| 2139 3 4 | 894 2 0 | 1183 19 3 | 982 14 8 | | |

# CONNAUGHT.

GALWAY.

| Names of Assistant Commissioners by whom Case was decided | No. | Name of Tenant | Name of Landlord | Townland |
|---|---|---|---|---|
| Assistant Commissioners— | | | | |
| M. T. OMAN (Legal). R. McCann. A. B. MONTGOMERY. | 6370 | Patrick Griffin, | Sir Henry Burke, Bart., | Knockavane, |
| | 6371 | Margaret Dillon (Pat), | do. | Monganstly, |
| | 6372 | Pat Ford, | Gerald Burke | Vert Brown, pt. of, |
| | 6373 | Pat Marrion, | do. | do. |
| | 6377 | John Ford, | do. | do. |
| | 6373 | Martin Smyth, | do. | do. |
| | 6379 | John Brown, | do. | do. |
| | 6380 | Michael Daly, | do. | do. |
| | 6381 | Bartholomew Donlon, | William O'Reilly, | Ellern, |
| | 6382 | Thomas Fallon, | do. | Ballinlass, |
| | 6383 | Timothy Boyle, | do. | do. |
| | 6384 | Patrick O'Connor, | do. | Killinney, |
| | 6385 | Edward Plunket, | do. | do. |
| | 6386 | Denis Fallon, | do. | Ballinlass, |
| | 6387 | Matthew Tierney, | do. | Carrokool, |
| | 6388 | Bridget Shaughnessy, | do. | Ellern, |
| | 6389 | Michael Mahlon, | George E. Dowling, | Tinard, |
| | 6390 | Michael O'Flaherty, | do. | Larias, |
| | 6391 | Bridget Brennan, | Digman, Minors, by Benjamin Whitney, their Guardian. | Ballaghanghig, East, |
| | 6392 | Patrick Mannell, | do. | do. |
| | 6393 | Michael Swift, | do. | do. |
| | 6394 | Martin Mulvehill, | John Digman | do. |
| | 6395 | Michael Banks, | do. | do. |

# TABLE OF JUDICIAL RENTS.

## GALWAY—continued.

| Amount of Holding, Statute. | Poor Law Valuation. | Former Rent. | Judicial Rent. | Observations. |
|---|---|---|---|---|
| A. R. P. | £ s. d. | £ s. d. | £ s. d. | |
| 14 2 0 | 5 15 0 | 4 16 0 | 3 16 0 | |
| 10 0 15 | 4 15 0 | 3 6 0 | 3 10 0 | |
| 26 0 31 | 0 15 0 | 7 10 0 | 5 6 0 | |
| 18 3 24 | 3 11 0 | 3 7 6 | 2 6 0 | |
| 18 3 36 | 3 10 0 | 3 7 6 | 3 6 0 | |
| 18 4 36 | 3 10 6 | 3 7 6 | 2 6 0 | |
| 6 3 37 | 3 6 0 | 3 10 0 | 1 15 0 | |
| 13 3 26 | 3 10 0 | 3 7 6 | 3 6 0 | |
| 26 1 9 | 13 4 0 | 16 0 0 | 10 16 0 | |
| 21 0 8 | 13 0 0 | 13 0 0 | 9 12 0 | |
| 13 3 61 | 6 16 0 | 7 6 0 | 5 10 0 | |
| 11 0 18 | 3 0 0 | 6 0 0 | 3 16 0 | |
| 11 1 81 | 4 0 0 | 4 0 0 | 3 18 0 | |
| 36 3 86 | 20 0 0 | 19 0 0 | 16 10 0 | Rent changed in 1860, from £13. |
| 16 3 22 | 7 0 0 | 7 0 0 | 5 10 0 | |
| 22 2 4 | 7 16 0 | 7 13 0 | 3 13 0 | |
| 17 1 6 | 8 15 0 | 9 7 6 | 7 7 0 | |
| 9 0 20 | 3 10 0 | 3 7 6 | 2 17 6 | |
| 11 1 17 | 3 6 0 | 3 15 0 | 3 6 0 | |
| 13 3 23 | 4 5 0 | 4 16 0 | 3 12 6 | |
| 11 3 6 | 3 0 6 | 3 7 0 | 3 11 6 | |
| 6 3 34 | 3 5 0 | 3 10 0 | 2 6 0 | |

| Names of Assistant Commissioners by whom Cases were decided. | No. | Name of Tenant. | Name of Landlord. |
|---|---|---|---|
| **Assistant Commissioners—** | | | |
| D. Tighe (Legal). | 4533 | Terence McGowan, | James Johnston, |
| O. Vanheldon. | 4033 | Henry Brennan, contd. in name of Robert J. Reynolds. | Lord John Massy, |
| B. Lindsay. | 4034 | Paul Fealy, | John Meehan, contd. to of Mary T. Meehan &c |
| | 4035 | Denis Chavy, | do. |
| | 4036 | Charles McGlade, | do. |
| | 4037 | Mary Rooney Limd. Admr. of Bryan Rooney. | do. |
| | 4038 | Bryan McDowy, | do. |
| | | | |
| **Assistant Commissioners—** | 4039 | Arthur Harrison, | Sir Gilbert King, Bart., |
| M. T. Cross (Legal). | 4040 | Do. | do. |
| W. J. Connolly. | 4041 | Mary Costello, | James R. Peyton, |
| J. Ryan. | 4042 | Patrick Flynn, | do. |
| | 4043 | Parrish Doran, | do. |
| | 4044 | John McWeeney, | do. |
| | 4045 | Michael Reynolds, | James Watson, |
| | 4046 | Juliana Wtford, | do. |
| | 4047 | John Moran, | do. |
| | 4048 | Ellen Doherty, Admrix of Michael Doherty. | Robert James Lloyd, |
| | 4049 | James Burke, | do. |
| | 4050 | James Fleming, | do. |
| | 4051 | James Doran, | do. |
| | 4052 | Patrick Boyle, | Francis O'Beirne, contd's tenms of Hugh O'Bely |
| | 4053 | Patrick McNulty, | do. |
| | 4054 | Patrick Mannion, | do. |
| | 4055 | John Harkin, | do. |
| | 4056 | Michael Mahon, | do. |
| | 4057 | Peter Mahon, | do. |
| | 4058 | John Godfrey, | do. |
| | 4059 | Mary Reynolds & ano., Reps.of Owen Scroggins. | Mrs. Mary Anne Am and another, |
| | 4060 | Morrison M. Taylor, | do. |
| | 4061 | Francis Dignam, | do. |
| | 4062 | Mary Keegan & ano., | do. |
| | 4063 | John Taylor, | do. |
| | 4064 | Dominick Flynn, | Owen Meehn, |

## LEITRIM.

| Extent of Holding, Acreds. | Poor Law Valuation. | Former Rent. | Judicial Rent. | Observations. | Value of Tenancy. |
|---|---|---|---|---|---|
| A. R. P. | £ s. d. | £ s. d. | £ s. d. | | £ s. d. |
| 6 3 2 | 3 15 0 | 8 17 8 | 8 0 0 | By consent. | |
| 30 8 85 | 37 15 0 | 36 0 0 | 25 0 0 | do. | |
| 13 6 0 | 8 0 0 | 4 8 0 | 3 17 8 | do. | |
| 6 3 31 | 3 15 0 | 4 0 0 | 3 13 4 | do. | |
| 21 3 25 | 7 15 0 | 11 16 0 | 7 10 0 | do. | |
| 49 0 28 | 14 10 0 | 33 4 0 | 14 0 0 | do. | |
| 19 8 82 | 6 10 0 | 0 1 0 | 6 0 0 | do. | |
| 17 2 31 | 0 15 0 | 13 6 0 | 9 15 0 | | |
| 34 1 34 | 15 5 0 | 15 3 1 | 13 0 0 | | |
| 16 0 29 | 11 10 0 | 11 9 6 | 10 0 0 | | |
| 24 1 7 | 8 15 0 | 11 0 8 | 9 0 0 | | |
| 18 0 4 | 8 0 0 | 3 18 5 | 8 6 0 | | |
| 6 3 20 | 3 15 0 | 3 16 10 | 3 15 0 | | |
| 28 3 34 | 13 0 0 | 16 2 8 | 11 0 0 | | |
| 18 3 30 | 4 10 0 | 6 11 8 | 4 5 0 | | |
| 63 0 30 | 6 8 0 | 8 13 8 | 6 0 0 | | |
| 38 0 30 | 8 10 0 | 10 28 0 | 8 5 0 | | |
| 14 8 2 | 6 0 0 | 7 8 0 | 5 18 0 | | |
| 16 3 14 | 4 0 0 | 6 8 0 | 4 0 0 | | |
| 32 6 16 | 8 2 0 | 7 0 0 | 6 8 0 | | |
| 6 3 0 | 3 0 6 | 6 0 0 | 1 5 0 | | |
| 13 0 20 | 10 8 0 | 10 15 0 | 0 0 0 | | |
| 14 1 30 | 0 0 0 | 0 19 6 | 8 0 0 | | |
| 1 3 38 | 0 15 6 | 1 0 0 | 0 15 0 | | |
| 11 0 10 | 8 18 0 | 6 0 0 | 1 0 0 | | |
| 10 8 8 | 3 17 0 | 6 0 0 | 3 18 0 | | |
| 9 3 23 | 4 6 0 | 8 12 6 | 6 10 0 | | |
| 35 1 82 | 18 6 0 | 14 16 7 | 8 0 0 | | |
| 65 0 11 | 15 15 0 | 13 10 7 | 13 0 0 | | |
| 26 1 8 | 7 8 0 | 7 7 6 | 6 0 0 | | |
| 70 0 36 | 7 0 0 | 8 3 10 | 5 10 8 | | |
| 60 0 8 | 18 10 0 | 10 0 0 | 15 0 0 | | |
| 8 1 0 | 3 5 0 | 3 0 0 | 3 0 0 | | |

| Names of Assistant Commissioners by whom cases were decided. | No. | Name of Tenant. | Name of Land |
|---|---|---|---|
| **Assistant Commissioners:—** | | | |
| M. T. Cross (Legal). | 4066 | Robert Mulroy, | ... | Captain O. R. Sim |
| W. J. Gorman. | 4066 | Thomas McElharry, | — | do. |
| J. Rice. | 4067 | Patrick Dolan, | — | do. |
| | 4068 | Michael McMorrow, | —, | do. |
| | 4069 | Patrick Maguire, | ... | Miss Eleanor J. C another |
| | 1070 | Francis Gibbon, | .— | Very Rev. A. W. |
| | 1071 | James Berry, | .— | George Marsham, |
| | 4072 | Patrick Gallogley, | —, | Landan de la P. O |
| | 4073 | Michael Gallagher, | —, | Captain J. F. Ter |
| | 4074 | Bridget Moran, | —, | Mrs. K. H. Simp |
| | 4075 | Patrick Feeney, | ... | Henry T. D. Ur another, Trustee R. Simpson. |
| | 4076 | Bernard Bohan, | — | Lord Southwell, |
| | 4077 | Patrick Johnston, | — | Robert Hamilton, |

27

## LEITRIM—continued.

| Acreage of Holding Statute | Poor Law Valuation | Former Rent | Judicial Rent | Observations | Value of Tenancy |
|---|---|---|---|---|---|
| A. R. P. | £ s. d. | £ s. d. | £ s. d. | | £ s. d. |
| 16 0 29 | 5 15 0 | 5 0 0 | 4 15 0 | Rent changed in 1853 from £5 10s. | |
| 8 2 15 | 7 0 0 | 6 0 0 | 5 19 6 | | |
| 13 0 34 | 9 10 0 | 6 0 0 | 3 6 0 | | |
| 31 0 29 | 11 0 0 | 11 10 0 | 8 10 0 | | |
| 33 1 20 | 8 15 0 | 10 0 0 | 7 10 0 | | |
| 65 3 12 | 16 5 0 | 18 0 0 | 16 10 0 | | |
| 51 1 20 | 19 10 0 | 20 0 0 | 16 0 0 | | |
| 3 0 24 | 3 10 0 | 4 5 0 | 3 5 0 | | |
| 23 3 8 | 9 0 5 | 11 9 0 | 6 0 0 | | |
| 19 0 0 | 15 10 0 | 12 10 0 | 11 10 0 | | |
| 16 0 26 | 11 10 0 | 10 15 0 | 8 16 5 | | |
| 10 1 30 | 6 6 0 | 6 0 0 | 6 0 0 | | |
| 15 1 16 | 6 6 0 | 5 17 2 | 6 0 0 | | |
| 1,000 0 2½ | 571 7 0 | 436 3 5 | 331 6 0 | | |

## ROSCOMMON.

| Names of Assistant Commissioners by whom Cases were decided. | No. | Name of Tenant. | Name of Landlord. |
|---|---|---|---|
| Assistant Commissioners— | | | |
| M. T. Green (Legal), J. MacW____, G. B. Belfour. | 5760 | Patrick Doherty, ... | Thomas O. W. Scott, trustees, by Henry L. J. his Guardian. |
| | 5761 | Martin Halvert, Rep. of Pat Halvert. | do. |
| | 5762 | Bridget Fannon, — | do. |
| | 5763 | Andrew Roderty, ... | do. |
| | 5764 | Martin Thomas, — | do. |
| | 5765 | Patrick Flynn, ... | do. |
| | 5766 | William McNein, — | do. |
| | 5767 | John Burns, ... | do. |
| | 5768 | Michael Kilbride, ... | do. |
| | 5769 | Matthew Walker, ... | do. |
| | 5770 | Michael Morris, ... | do. |
| | 5771 | Thomas Scatchwell, — | do. |
| | 5772 | John McKin, — | do. |
| | 5773 | Robert McManoway, — | do. |
| | 5774 | Herbert Thos, — | do. |
| | 5775 | Thomas Conway, — | do. |
| | 5776 | Robert Scatchwell, ... | do. |
| | 5777 | Do., — | do. |
| | 5778 | Patrick Kirwan, — | do. |
| | 5779 | Michael Geary, ... | do. |
| | 5780 | John Ost, ... | do. |
| | 5781 | William McParlan, — | do. |
| | 5782 | Ellen Hart, Rep. of Bernard Hart. | do. |
| | 5783 | Thomas Gregg, — | do. |
| | 5784 | Michael Simpson, ... | do. |
| | 5785 | Patrick Kennedy, ... | do. |
| | 5786 | John Doherty, ... | do. |
| | 5787 | Martin Rodgers, — | do. |
| | 5788 | Mary Walker, — | do. |
| | 5789 | William Carroll, ... | do. |
| | 5790 | Edward Gallagher, ... | do. |
| | 5791 | James McNern, — | do. |
| | 5792 | Owen Tighe, — | do. |
| | 5793 | Catherine Kenney, — | do. |

ROSCOMMON—*continued.*

| Extent of Holding Statute. | Poor Law Valuation. | Former Rent. | Judicial Rent. | Observations. | Value of Tenancy. |
|---|---|---|---|---|---|
| A. R. P. | £ s. d. | £ s. d. | £ s. d. | | £ s. d. |
| 13 0 0 | 8 15 0 | 4 3 0 | 3 5 0 | | |
| 11 2 10 | 4 5 0 | 5 2 0 | 5 5 0 | | |
| 7 1 20 | 8 10 0 | 7 10 0 | 6 10 0 | | |
| 7 0 0 | 4 0 0 | 8 5 4 | 5 0 0 | | |
| 15 0 20 | 8 15 0 | 4 10 0 | 1 0 0 | | |
| 11 0 0 | 7 0 0 | 8 5 0 | 2 0 0 | | |
| 22 1 35 | 5 5 0 | 6 5 0 | 5 10 0 | | |
| 7 3 01 | 3 0 0 | 3 5 0 | 2 5 0 | | |
| 22 2 20 | 10 0 0 | 10 15 10 | 7 10 0 | | |
| 18 0 15 | 14 5 0 | 15 5 5 | 9 17 0 | | |
| 5 0 0 | 2 5 0 | 5 14 6 | 3 5 0 | | |
| 40 1 33 | 17 15 0 | 19 7 0 | 15 12 0 | | |
| 15 2 0 | 4 15 0 | 4 8 0 | 3 10 0 | | |
| 63 3 15 | 54 15 0 | 61 3 5 | 52 0 0 | | |
| 10 0 0 | 4 5 0 | 5 0 0 | 4 0 0 | | |
| 5 0 20 | 4 15 0 | 5 5 4 | 5 12 0 | | |
| 16 1 05 | 5 5 0 | 11 4 5 | 8 0 0 | Rent changed in 1871 from ... 15 0 0 £ s. d. | |
| 11 0 0 | 5 12 0 | 7 5 5 | 5 10 0 | | |
| 4 3 27 | 1 15 0 | 3 5 0 | 1 15 0 | 1851, 3 5 0 | |
| 7 3 33 | 3 0 0 | 5 0 5 | 3 5 0 | do. 2 5 5 | |
| 5 1 33 | 2 5 0 | 1 5 0 | 2 5 5 | do. 5 15 0 | |
| 11 5 17 | 4 3 0 | 5 0 0 | 5 0 5 | 1850, 7 14 0 | |
| 5 5 0 | 5 5 0 | 5 5 5 | 2 10 0 | | |
| 7 0 0 | 5 0 0 | 5 0 0 | 5 10 0 | do. 7 10 0 | |
| 4 3 0 | 4 0 0 | 5 5 0 | 4 5 0 | | |
| 5 1 15 | 1 10 0 | 5 5 0 | 3 0 0 | | |
| 12 5 16 | 5 0 0 | 5 5 5½ | 4 10 0 | | |
| 25 0 20 | 7 5 0 | 10 5 2 | 8 0 0 | | |
| 5 1 5 | 0 10 0 | 0 19 0 | 0 19 0 | | |
| 1 5 20 | 2 0 0 | 2 0 0 | 1 0 0 | | |
| 5 1 0 | 5 5 0 | 5 0 0 | 4 5 0 | do. 7 0 0 | |
| 7 0 15 | 2 15 0 | 3 5 0 | 2 5 0 | | |
| 3 1 0 | 3 0 0 | 4 10 0 | 3 10 0 | | |
| 13 1 5 | 3 0 0 | 3 0 5 | 3 5 0 | do. 4 5 0 | |

COUNTY OF

| Name of Assistant Commissioners by whom Cases were decided. | No. | Name of Tenant. | Name of Landlord. | Townland. |
|---|---|---|---|---|
| Assistant Commissioners—<br>M. T. Cben (Legal).<br>J. MacHugh.<br>G. S. Stewart. | 5784 | Michael Halbert, ... | Thomas G. W. Sandford, a minor, by Henry L. Jephson, his Guardian. | Ballindrimin, ... |
| | 5785 | John Hynes, — | do. | do. |
| | 5796 | Dominic Healy, — | do. | do. |
| | 5797 | Patrick McDonnell, ... | do. | Mass, |
| | 5784 | James Clogher, — | do. | do. |
| | 5799 | Francis Dolan, Limd. Administrator of James Dolan. | do. | do. |
| | 5800 | Patrick Burke, — | do. | do. |
| | 5801 | Thomas Coffey, ... | do. | do. |
| | 5802 | Martin Forde, — | do. | do. |
| | 5803 | Thomas Doherty, — | do. | Ballindrimin, |
| | 5804 | Daniel McLoughlin, — | do. | do. |
| | 5805 | Stephen Tims, — | do. | do. |
| | 5806 | Martin Doherty, — | do. | do. |
| | 5807 | John Flynn, — | do. | do. |
| | 5808 | John Mahon, — | do. | do. |
| | 5809 | Andrew Casey, ... | do. | do. |
| | 5810 | William Birchwell, — | do. | Ardeen, |
| | 5811 | John Murray, — | do. | — |
| | 5812 | Charles Glavin, — | do. | Ardeen, |
| | 5813 | Nicholas Abbott, ... | do. | Tawnes, |
| | 5814 | Martin Morris, — | do. | Turrantaes, |
| | 5815 | John Glover, junior, — | do. | Mass, |
| | 5816 | Godfrey Clarke, ... | do. | Turrantaes, |
| | 5817 | Do. — | do. | do |
| | 5818 | Hubert Birchwell, — | do. | Ardeen, |
| | 5819 | Do. ... | do. | Turrantaes, |
| | 5820 | Thomas Birchwell, — | do. | do. |
| | 5821 | Patrick Coffey, ... | do. | Mass, |
| | 5822 | Michael G. Sweeney, ... | do. | Closerus, |
| | | | | Total, |

## ROSCOMMON—*continued*.

| Extent of Holding. Statute | Poor Law Valuation. | Former Rent. | Judicial Rent. | Observations. |
|---|---|---|---|---|
| A. R. P. | £ s. d. | £ s. d. | £ s. d. | |
| 13 1 0 | 5 3 0 | 6 0 0 | 3 0 0 | |
| 4 1 10 | 1 4 0 | 3 9 2 | 1 15 0 | |
| 14 5 0 | 4 0 0 | 5 0 11 | 3 0 11 | |
| 13 0 20 | 5 10 0 | 6 7 0 | 5 10 0 | |
| 19 1 30 | 5 16 0 | 6 13 0 | 3 6 0 | |
| 51 3 0 | 9 5 0 | 13 0 0 | 8 0 0 | |
| 17 0 20 | 7 0 0 | 9 18 10 | 6 0 0 | |
| 31 0 10 | 5 5 0 | 6 7 1 | 4 4 0 | |
| 17 0 0 | 6 5 0 | 8 11 4 | 5 13 0 | |
| 20 1 20 | 6 0 0 | 10 19 4 | 5 6 0 | |
| 11 0 0 | 1 10 0 | 3 14 0 | 2 0 0 | |
| 13 3 10 | 10 0 0 | 18 2 6 | 9 10 0 | |
| 6 0 20 | 8 5 0 | 3 1 3 | 7 12 0 | |
| 10 1 20 | 6 10 0 | 4 10 0 | 3 10 0 | |
| 7 2 0 | 1 14 0 | 1 17 6 | 1 4 0 | |
| 20 0 20 | 9 6 0 | 11 10 4 | 8 15 0 | |
| 23 3 30 | 19 6 0 | 17 15 0 | 18 0 0 | |
| 10 0 0 | 2 0 0 | 6 6 0 | 3 0 0 | |
| 23 0 17 | 18 10 0 | 20 14 6 | 16 0 0 | |
| 14 1 20 | 6 18 0 | 9 9 0 | 7 10 0 | |
| 6 1 0 | 3 6 0 | 3 3 0 | 3 14 0 | |
| 20 3 2 | 6 10 0 | 7 0 0 | 6 0 0 | |
| 31 0 0 | 12 10 0 | 20 0 0 | 11 5 0 | |
| 43 1 37 | 20 6 0 | 31 7 8 | 16 10 0 | |
| 63 2 2 | 61 10 0 | 46 0 0 | 57 3 0 | Rent changed in 1848 £ s. d. from . . . 57 0 0 |
| 13 3 11 | 6 10 0 | 9 7 6 | 6 15 6 | |
| 15 1 37 | 11 3 0 | 11 0 0 | 7 18 0 | |
| 13 0 0 | 6 15 0 | 6 0 0 | 4 15 0 | |

PROVINCE OF

COUNTY OF

| Name of Assistant Commissioners by which Cases were decided. | No. | Name of Tenant. | Name of Landlord. | Townland. |
|---|---|---|---|---|
| Assistant Commissioners —<br><br>J. R. Green, q.c. (Legal).<br>J. J. Quirk.<br>J. Martin. | 5180 | John Corbett, ... | Cornelius Killeen, | Ballymakeshog |
| | 5181 | Johanna King, ... | Julia Haugh, ... | Dunabeg, |
| | 5182 | James Brown, | Mrs. Mary Foley, | Derrylough, |
| | 5183 | Margaret Talty, | Richard Griffith, | Doolagh, |
| | 5184 | Patrick Hassett, | Richard Sharpcole, | Tullahern. |
| | 5185 | John Walsh, | do. | Carrowbloghmore, |
| | | | | Total, — |

COUNTY OF

| Head Commission. | 5621 | Bartholomew Coleman, | Jane Cuthbert and others, ... | Rathbeg, — |
|---|---|---|---|---|

COUNTY OF

# MUNSTER.

## CLARE.

| Amount of Holding in Acres | Poor Law Valuation | Former Rent | Judicial Rent | Observations | Value of Tenancy |
|---|---|---|---|---|---|
| A. R. P. | £ s. d. | £ s. d. | £ s. d. | | £ s. d. |
| 0 2 20 | tenant claimed | 1 0 0 | 1 0 0 | | |
| 1 3 13 | do. | 1 4 0 | 1 0 0 | | |
| 3 2 0 | 1 4 0 | 4 7 0 | 3 13 0 | By consent | |

## COUNTY OF

| Names of Assistant Commissioners by whom Cases were decided. | No. | Name of Tenant. | Name of Landlord. | Townland. |
|---|---|---|---|---|
| **Assistant Commissioners—** | | | | |
| J. S. Green, Q.C. (Legal). | 2353 | John Ryan, ... | William H. M. Bennett, | Coolnevough, |
| J. Harrington. | 2354 | Mary Dwellen, Limd. Adml. of Philip Davidson | Charles W. Smith. | Gallson, South, |
| J. J. O'Shaughnessy. | 2355 | Denis Keogn Limd Adml. of Johanna Dwyer. | do. | do. |
| | 2356 | Michael O'Brien, Limd. Admr. of Jeremiah O'Brien | Lord Henry. | Coolananbawen, |
| | 2357 | Edward Kiely, | do. | Kilglass, |
| | 2358 | Do. | do. | do. |
| | 2359 | Do. | do. | Coolmaslagra, |
| | 2360 | Do. | do. | do. |
| | 2361 | Thomas Scully, | do. | Deerpark, |
| | 2362 | James Brennan and anor., | Count de Salis, | Loughgur, |
| | 2363 | Thomas Bailey, | do. | do. |
| | 2364 | Patrick Daly, | do. | Knockraw, |
| | 2365 | Patrick Dooley (Fett), | do. | Rashaun, |
| | 2366 | Patrick O'Brien and anor., | do. | Loughgur, |
| | 2367 | Thomas Dwyer, | do. | do. |
| | 2368 | Thomas Carroll, | do. | do. |
| | 2369 | Edward Garvy, | do. | do. |
| | 2370 | John McNamara, | do. | do. |
| | 2371 | Nicholas Hayes, | do. | do. |
| | 2372 | John Daly and another, | do. | do. |
| | 2373 | Thomas Hickey, | do. | do. |
| | | | | Total, |

## COUNTY OF

| Assistant Commissioners— | No. | Name of Tenant | Name of Landlord | Townland |
|---|---|---|---|---|
| J. H. Edge (Legal). | 5356 | Jeremiah Power, | H. E. J. Larum, | Rusebe, West, |
| F. M. Gannon. | 3537 | Mary Walsh, | Thomas Brien, | Ballykeigan, |
| H. G. Pery. | 3538 | Bridget Landy | Barbara J. Murray, | Ballydavid, |
| | 3539 | Bridget Slattery. | Averina M. Rende, | Bawnavroste, |
| | 3540 | Mary Walsh. | John Vaughan, | Poulacapple, |
| | 3541 | Edmund Butler, Exor. of Jantre Hackett | Rev. R. R. Wright, rector in name of Miss E. R. Wright, | Mullinahy and another, Followathen, |
| | 3542 | Denis Hall, | Benjamin C. Henbury, | |

**LIMERICK—continued.**

| Extent of Holding. Acres. | Poor Law Valuation. | Former Rent. | Judicial Rent. | Observations. | Valued Tenancy. |
|---|---|---|---|---|---|
| A. R. P. | £ s. d. | £ s. d. | £ s. d. | | £ s. d. |
| 20 0 17 | 16 0 0 | 13 8 6 | 10 0 0 | | |
| 1 0 27 | 3 5 6 | 2 18 6 | 1 16 0 | | |
| 1 6 20 | 1 10 6 | 2 0 0 | 1 0 0 | | |
| 10 1 13 | 6 0 0 | 6 0 0 | 4 16 0 | | |
| 11 0 25 | 3 15 0 | 4 13 0 | 4 15 0 | | |
| 46 0 13 | 22 15 0 | 19 15 6 | 20 0 0 | | |
| 9 1 14 | 1 0 0 | 3 18 0 | 2 0 0 | | |
| 24 1 30 | 10 0 0 | 18 7 0 | 13 0 0 | | |
| 10 3 11 | 8 5 0 | 11 0 0 | 8 10 0 | And right of grazing on herdsbury on adjoining mountain. | |
| 11 0 23 | 11 15 0 | 15 14 7 | 11 0 0 | By consent. | |
| 6 1 24 | 6 10 0 | 7 15 9 | 5 0 0 | do. | |
| 13 0 3 | 10 0 0 | 14 0 0 | 9 10 0 | do. | |
| 13 0 6 | 11 10 0 | 18 8 0 | 18 0 0 | do. | |
| 7 1 6 | 4 10 0 | 7 4 4 | 6 0 0 | do. | |
| 6 3 10 | 7 15 0 | 11 19 1 | 7 10 0 | do. | |
| 9 1 64 | 7 5 0 | 17 0 0 | 8 0 0 | do. | |
| 19 3 13 | 8 10 0 | 14 5 0 | 16 0 0 | do. | |
| 6 3 20 | 7 3 0 | 13 10 0 | 8 0 0 | do. | |
| 6 3 21 | 7 16 0 | 8 16 2 | 7 0 0 | do. | |
| 3 0 55 | 3 0 0 | 6 0 0 | 5 16 0 | do. | |
| 6 1 25 | 6 0 0 | 6 16 3 | 4 0 0 | do. | |
| 449 2 6 | 663 0 0 | 622 15 6 | 479 10 0 | | |

**TIPPERARY.**

| | | |
|---|---|---|
| ham Pollard, | ... | do. | — |
| a Power, Admix. of han Power. | do. | — |
| a Tobin, | ... | do. | — |
| a McGrath, | ... | do. | ... |
| liam McGrath, | ... | do. | ... |
| Do., ... | ... | do. | ... |
| Do., ... | ... | do. | ... |
| igan Egan, | — | O. V. Montgomery and Trustees of Will of V A. Tisdall. | |
| a Lanigan, | ... | do. | — |
| mas Power, | ... | John G. Pennell and | |
| y Delany, | ... | Colonel F. K. B. Tighe | |
| a Brennan, | ... | do. | — |
| a Agnew, | ... | George Langley, ... | |
| am Nim, consigned, in name of Mary Murray. | William A. Grdng, a by Annbelle Unio Guardian. | | |
| de McGrath, | — | do. | ... |
| mas B. O'Mahony, | ... | Georgina Cohen, | |
| Grady, | ... | Samuel Perry, | ... |
| rick Chetwell, | ... | Mrs. Caroline Shaw, | |
| rick Daly, | ... | Stephen Moore, | |
| a O'Neill, | ... | William M. Constable, | |
| huel O'Brien | and | Rebecca Barfield and | |

## TIPPERARY—continued.

| Extent of Holding. Statute Acres. | Poor Law Valuation. | Former Rent. | Judicial Rent. | Observations. | Value of Tenancy. |
|---|---|---|---|---|---|
| A. R. P. | £ s. d. | £ s. d. | £ s. d. | | £ s. d. |
| 55 2 20 | 19 0 0 | 81 14 8 | 21 15 0 | | |
| 86 1 9 | 55 10 0 | 76 17 0 | 53 0 0 | | |
| 9 0 0 | 7 0 0 | 9 0 0 | 1 10 0 | | |
| 21 3 20 | 16 5 0 | 17 0 0 | 19 10 0 | | |
| 23 1 25 | 20 10 0 | 20 0 0 | 17 10 0 | | |
| 51 1 20 | 28 10 0 | 52 0 0 | 28 10 0 | | |
| 62 1 35 | 45 17 0 | 58 0 10 | 51 0 0 | | |
| 4 3 18 | 2 10 0 | 9 0 0 | 3 0 0 | | |
| 19 0 10 | 15 5 0 | 18 10 0 | 18 10 0 | | |
| 11 2 0 | 4 15 0 | 9 5 0 | 8 0 0 | | |
| 14 0 20 | 9 10 0 | 11 7 0 | 9 0 0 | | |
| 7 2 4 | 4 0 0 | 9 15 4 | 8 15 4 | | |
| 11 2 9 | 10 5 0 | 7 10 9 | 7 10 9 | | |
| 8 3 22 | 5 15 0 | 6 17 8 | 6 0 0 | | |
| 45 0 19 | 31 0 0 | 38 10 1 | 30 0 0 | | |
| 21 3 35 | 23 5 0 | 53 10 0 | 16 0 0 | | |
| 18 1 4 | 13 0 0 | 15 10 0 | 13 10 0 | | |
| 101 2 11 | 43 5 0 | 60 3 10 | 51 0 0 | | |
| 20 1 0 | 13 10 0 | 15 0 0 | 12 0 0 | | |
| 40 1 3 | 21 0 0 | 23 0 0 | 22 0 0 | | |
| 33 3 25 | 23 5 0 | 22 0 0 | 20 10 0 | | |
| 13 3 0 | 10 3 0 | 10 10 0 | 8 10 0 | | |

# CIVIL BILL

## PROVINCE OF

### COUNTY OF

| No. | Name of Tenant. | Name of Landlord. | Townland. |
|---|---|---|---|
| 1633 | Allen Magee, | Rev. Thomas Moore, | Killesa, |
| 1634 | Peter MaKenn, | Daniel Gallimore, | Ballynamery, |
| 1635 | Philip Martin, | George Raymond, | Carvereley, |
| 1636 | Charles Reilly, | James Graham, | Drummon, |
| 1637 | James Smith, | Miss Margaret Spere, | Derryloghan, |
| 1638 | Mary A. Hamilton, Rep. of Francis Hamilton. | Countess Morley and another, | Corkel. |
| 1639 | James Sullivan, | Lady Garragh, | Seerem, |
| 1640 | Patrick Clarke, | do. | Legland, |
| 1641 | Jane Maxwell, Rep. of Alexander Maxwell. | do. | Tullylackan, |
| 1642 | John Bell, | John G. Jones, | Dromcran, |
| 1643 | Pat McMahon, | Augustus Henkell and anor., | Dromaho. |
| 1644 | James McMahon, Junior, | do. | do. |
| 1645 | John McCabe, | Rem R. G. M. Talbot and ors., | Drommarrow, |
| 1646 | Patrick Dober, | Mrs. Olivia Ratrney & anor., | Killabandrish, |
| 1647 | Robert McGovern, | Sampson H. Maxwell, | Oredun, |
| 1648 | John Osgrove, | Trustees of James Carney, | Sharry, |
| 1649 | William Rewist, | Mrs. Josephine Kelly, | Serum, |
| 1650 | Thomas Lynch, | William H. Brthbornes, | Clonarvale, |
| 1651 | Philip Reilly, Rep. of Owen Reilly. | Edward J. Saunderson, | Carrickmamadon |
| 1652 | Thomas Murray and anor., Reps. of Michael Murray, decesed. | do. | do. |
| 1653 | Charles McCabe & anor., | James F. Frahter, | Derryhum, |
|  |  |  | Total. |

# COURTS.

## ULSTER.

### CAVAN.

| Name of Holding, Return | | | Poor Law Valuation | | | Present Rent | | |
|---|---|---|---|---|---|---|---|---|
| A. | R. | P. | £ | s. | d. | £ | s. | d. |
| 7 | 0 | 5 | 4 | 5 | 0 | 5 | 10 | 0 |
| 15 | 3 | 11 | 11 | 10 | 0 | 10 | 10 | 0 |
| 10 | 3 | 57 | 7 | 10 | 0 | 5 | 15 | 10 |
| 10 | 1 | 33 | 8 | 10 | 0 | 7 | 10 | 3 |
| 19 | 0 | 21 | 13 | 5 | 0 | 13 | 7 | 5 |
| 25 | 1 | 16 | 8 | 0 | 0 | 7 | 14 | 7 |
| 77 | 3 | 93 | 13 | 5 | 0 | 13 | 10 | 0 |
| 6 | 1 | 22 | 7 | 16 | 0 | 3 | 0 | 0 |
| 11 | 3 | 5 | 8 | 3 | 0 | 7 | 9 | 6 |
| 13 | 1 | 1 | 9 | 15 | 0 | 8 | 17 | 6 |
| 9 | 0 | 0 | 7 | 5 | 0 | 7 | 10 | 0 |
| 17 | 0 | 11 | 13 | 0 | 0 | 11 | 16 | 4 |
| 11 | 0 | 31 | 9 | 15 | 0 | 11 | 0 | 0 |
| 38 | 3 | 13 | 71 | 10 | 0 | 19 | 0 | 0 |
| 16 | 3 | 2 | 10 | 0 | 0 | 10 | 0 | 0 |

CIVIL BILL COURTS

COUNTY OF

| Name of Tenant. | Name of Landlord. | Townland. |
|---|---|---|
| John Campbell, ... | Rupert F. Colclar, ... | Drumslon, ... |
| Bridget Swift, — | Acheson H. Irwin, — | Mullaraddy, — |
| | | Total, ... |

# PROVINCE OF

COUNTY OF

| Mary Doyle, ... | Fairwood Rynd, ... | Robertside, — |
|---|---|---|
| Patrick Dunne, ... | Lord Valentia, ... | Drananstown, — |
| | | Total, — |

COUNTY OF

## FERMANAGH.

| Extent of Holding. Statute. | Poor Law Valuation. | Former Rent. | Judicial Rent. | Observations. |
|---|---|---|---|---|
| A. R. P. | £ s. d. | £ s. d. | £ s. d. | |
| 68 0 18 | 60 0 0 | 43 10 7 | 36 19 0 | |
| 10 6 20 | — | 7 16 11 | 6 10 6 | |
| 68 3 28 | 60 0 0 | 51 7 6 | 42 9 6 | |

# LEINSTER.

## KILDARE.

| | | | | |
|---|---|---|---|---|
| 9 0 38 | 2 10 0 | 6 0 0 | 2 0 0 | |
| 148 3 15 | 73 0 0 | 73 0 0 | 70 0 0 | |
| 153 3 15 | 77 10 0 | 79 0 0 | 73 0 0 | |

## KILKENNY.

| | | | | |
|---|---|---|---|---|
| 67 1 21 | 67 0 0 | 85 0 0 | 38 0 0 | |

## COUNTY.

COUNTY OF

| County Court Judge. | No. | Name of Tenant | Name of Landlord | Townland. |
|---|---|---|---|---|
| GERALD FITZGERALD | 774 | Theodore Kellett, — | Lord Decies, — | Newcastle, — |
| | 775 | Patrick Austin, ... | Hon. H. L. B. Rowley, ... | Clonlogan, — |
| | | | | Total, — |

QUEENS

| T. De Moleyns, Q.C. | 12 | Martin Donohoe, — | The Misses McNeale, ... | Killbride, — |

COUNTY OF

| William F. Darley, Q.C. | 6 | Maria Doran and others, | Viscount Bridport and anor., Trustees of Marquis of Devonshire. | Haylands, .. |
| | 7 | Do. — ... | do. — .. | do. — |
| | 8 | Do. — — | do. — — | do. — |
| | | | | Total, — |

MEATH .

| Census of Holding, Statute. | Poor Law Valuation. | Former Rent. | Judicial Rent. | Observations. |
|---|---|---|---|---|
| A. R. P. | £ s. d. | £ s. d. | £ s. d. | |
| 215 0 30 | 170 5 0 | 173 0 4 | 145 0 0 | |
| 11 1 10 | 7 0 0 | 7 15 10 | 5 0 0 | |
| 220 0 0 | 177 5 0 | 180 16 2 | 150 0 0 | |

COUNTY.

| | | | | |
|---|---|---|---|---|
| 53 0 0 | 23 0 0 | 28 0 6 | 17 0 0 | |

WICKLOW.

| | | | | |
|---|---|---|---|---|
| 11 1 16 | 6 5 0 | 16 0 0 | 11 10 0 | |
| 75 1 0 | 20 0 0 | 22 0 0 | 20 0 0 | |
| 15 1 31 | 6 5 0 | 16 0 0 | 10 17 0 | |
| 19 0 7 | 22 10 0 | 44 0 0 | 42 7 0 | |

# CONNAUGHT.

MAYO.

| County Court Judge. | No. | Name of Tenant. | Name of Landlord. | Townland. |
|---|---|---|---|---|
| J. H. Richardson | 3257 | Julia Feighan, | — Marquis of Sligo, — | — Carrowreagh, ... |
| | 3258 | James Rourke, | — Colonel J. P. Brabazon, | ... Rathnamlea, — |
| | 3259 | Thomas Walsh and others, | Blanhot. O. Allen and others, | Ospillaha, — |
| | 3260 | John Mowra, | ... Charles L. Fitzgerald, | ... Townalmeen, — |
| | 3261 | Philip Waldron, | — Colonel John P. Brabazon, — | Cabir, — |
| | 3262 | Brady Mulderrig, | — Robert W. Oram, | ... Ouruhrish, — |
| | 3263 | Thomas Lavin, | ... St. George Stock, ... | ... Lecarrowtemple, |
| | 3264 | Thomas Conghvey, | — Mosher's Estate and another, | Ballygavry, — |
| | 3266 | Pat Hyme, senior and junior, | do. | — do. — |
| | 3266 | Joseph Gaurican, | — Mrs. H. O'Malley, | ... Milnbosh, .. |
| | 3267 | Michael Ourley, | — Lord Dillon, — | — Corclesha, — |
| | 6716 | John Walsh, | — George R. Browne, | — Gavlhay, .. |
| | 3269 | Do., | do. — | — do. — |
| | | | | Total, — |

PROVINCE OF

MAYO—*continued.*

| Area of Holdings Statute. | Poor Law Valuation. | Former Rent. | Judicial Rent. | Observations. | Value of Tenancy |
|---|---|---|---|---|---|
| a. r. p. | £ s. d. | £ s. d. | £ s. d. | | |
| unascertained, | 5 0 0 | 8 10 0 | 3 0 0 | | |
| 18 1 13 | 6 10 0 | 7 19 4 | 6 6 0 | | |
| 21 2 37 | 5 15 0 | 8 10 5 | 8 0 0 | | |
| unascertained, | 2 7 6 | 3 6 0 | 3 8 0 | | |
| 19 0 0 | 5 10 0 | 11 9 9 | 8 0 0 | | |
| unascertained, | 4 17 0 | 9 0 0 | 8 5 0 | | |
| 12 2 8 | 2 0 0 | 6 0 0 | 4 10 0 | | |
| 3 8 0 | 3 0 0 | 3 0 8 | 3 5 0 | | |
| 4 0 0 | 2 16 0 | 4 3 3 | 3 5 0 | | |
| 7 0 23 | 1 10 0 | 3 0 0 | 1 16 0 | | |
| 50 1 0 | 12 0 0 | 14 0 0 | 12 0 0 | | |
| 8 2 0 | 3 0 0 | 4 10 0 | 3 0 0 | | |
| 4 5 0 | unascertained, | 1 0 0 | 1 0 0 | | |
| 173 0 37 | 91 0 0 | 107 16 11 | 80 13 0 | | |

# MUNSTER.

| County Court Judge. | No | Name of Tenant. | Name of Landlord. | Townland. |
|---|---|---|---|---|
| J. F. Hamilton, q.c. | 450 | John Sullivan, ... | Rev. John W. Neligan and another. | Knockaunbally, |
| | 451 | Maurice Spillane, ... | do. ... ... | Killeens, |
| | | | | Total, ... |

| William Andrews, q.c. | 233 | James Kennedy, ... | William D. Parter, | Killalla, |
|---|---|---|---|---|
| | 234 | Robert E. Going, ... | Henry Eustace, ... | Ballynamagh Torrent. |
| | | | | Total, ... |

Rents fixed upon the Reports of Valuers appointed by the Irish

# PROVINCE OF

| Number. | Name of Tenant. | Name of Landlord. | Townland. |
|---|---|---|---|
| 5 | Andrew Reid, ... | Lord Rathdonnell, | Tullybenny. |

# PROVINCE OF

## CORK.

| Extent of Holding. Acreate. | Poor Law Valuation. | Former Rent. | Judicial Rent. | Observations. | |
|---|---|---|---|---|---|
| A. R. P. | £ s. d. | £ s. d. | £ s. d. | | |
| 13 0 0 | 36 10 0 | 44 3 8 | 35 0 0 | | |
| 23 0 0 | 28 3 0 | 33 6 5 | 23 0 0 | | |
| 85 0 0 | 64 13 0 | 79 8 9 | 58 0 0 | | |

## TIPPERARY.

| 30 3 3 | 14 0 0 | 14 5 6 | 12 10 0 | |
|---|---|---|---|---|
| 123 2 18 | 92 15 0 | 112 11 10 | 115 0 0 | |
| 154 1 31 | 106 15 0 | 156 17 4 | 127 10 0 | |

## Land Commission on the Joint Application of Landlords and Tenants.

# ULSTER.

## MONAGHAN.

| Extent of Holding. Statute. | Poor Law Valuation. | Former Rent. | Judicial Rent. | Observations. |
|---|---|---|---|---|
| A. R. P. | £ s. d. | £ s. d. | £ s. d. | |
| 4 3 11 | 6 5 0 | 7 0 0 | 6 15 0 | |

# MUNSTER.

## CLARE.

LAND LAW (IRELAND) ACT, 1887.

LEASEHOLDERS.

# PROVINCE OF

## COUNTY OF

| Name of Assistant Commissioners by whom Cases were settled. | No. | Name of Tenant. | Name of Landlord. | Townland. |
|---|---|---|---|---|
| HEAD COMMISSION. | 1561 | Robert Wardekie, sued in name of John Maconghey and others. | Mrs. Jane Dunlop, ... | Gortmoney, ... |
| | 1562 | Colonel John McDonnell, | Earl of Antrim, ... | Kilmore, ... |
| | 1563 | John Mallroy, ... | John Chestnut and another, | Broughshane, ... |
| | 1564 | Samuel Moore, ... | Andrew McIlwraith, ... | Ballysalbane, — |
| | 1565 | John Young and another, Reps. of George Mid-Casdan. | Lord O'Neill, ... | Barnish, - |
| | 1566 | Do. ... ... | do. — | Magherough, - |
| Assistant Commissioners— | 1567 | John McMichael, | Kathleen Isabel Boyd, ... | Drummavaley, ... |
| E. Gibbs (Legal). J. Weir. L. W. Byers. | | | | Total, — |

## COUNTY OF

# ULSTER.

## ANTRIM.

| Tenant of Holding. Estate | Poor Law Valuation. | Former Rent. | Judicial Rent. | Observations. | Value of Tenancy |
|---|---|---|---|---|---|
| A. R. P. | £ s. d. | £ s. d. | £ s. d. | | £ s. d. |
| 37 0 0 | 13 5 0 | 19 0 0 | 16 0 0 | | |
| | | | | | |
| 141 0 21 | 117 15 0 | 107 0 0 | 78 0 0 | | |
| 21 1 5 | 15 5 0 | 23 12 1 | 16 12 6 | | |
| 17 3 35 | unappropriated | 16 5 0 | 9 1 0 | | |
| 13 3 4 | 54 15 0 | 51 8 5 | 53 15 5 | | |
| 103 2 15 | 139 10 0 | 58 18 8 | 65 5 0 | | |
| | | | | | |
| | | | | | |
| 78 1 34 | 48 0 0 | 83 0 0 | 42 15 0 | | |
| | | | | | |
| 400 3 35 | 390 10 0 | 347 18 5 | 870 18 0 | | |

| Name of Assistant Commissioners by whom Case was decided. | No. | Name of Tenant. | Name of Landlord. |
|---|---|---|---|
| HEAD COMMISSION. | 350 | Patrick Maguire, assisted by John Maguire, his brother-in-law. | Lyndon Bolton, — |
|  | 351 | Michael Donohoe, ... | do. — |

| Name of Assistant Commissioners by whom Case was decided. | No. | Name of Tenant. | Name of Landlord. |
|---|---|---|---|
| HEAD COMMISSION. | 351 | Thomas Crockett, — | Lord Templemore, |
| Assistant Commissioners — | 352 | Charles Chalmers, ... | George Irwin, — |
| D. Tierney (Legal). H. Jephson. O. Vanmarte. | 353 | Rev. Robert Beattie, Exor. of John Mortland. | Alfred G. Hastings, |
| D. Tierney (Legal). R. B. Houston. R. O'Reilly. | 354 | Samuel Graham, — | Bishop of Derry and others of the Mussenden Elise Graham, ... |
|  | 355 | Mathew Kilpatrick, — |  |
|  | 356 | David Williams, — | Viscount Southwell, Trustees of Southwell, a minor. |
|  | 357 | Catherine McCabb, — | Captain John Leslie, |
|  | 358 | Anthony Cullen, — | do. — |
|  | 359 | William Montgomery, | Samuel Saunderson, |
|  | 360 | Do., ... — | do. — |
|  | 361 | Robert McMorris, — | do. ... |

| | | | | | |
|---|---|---|---|---|---|
| 8 | 0 | 0 | 4 | 26 | |
| 60 | 10 | 0 | 58 | 0 | |
| | | | | | |
| 12 | 0 | 0 | 13 | 0 | |
| 54 | 4 | 8 | 45 | 18 | |
| 54 | 3 | 0 | 44 | 3 | |

# IRISH LAND COMMISSION.

COUNTY OF

| Name of Assistant Commissioners by whom Cases were decided. | No. | Name of Tenant. | Name of Landlord. | Townland. |
|---|---|---|---|---|
| Assistant Commissioners : | | | | |
| E. Grant (Legal). | 632 | Thomas McWilliams, | Sir David Taylor, | Ballygowan, |
| R. Garland | 634 | Do. | do. | do. |
| H. Coleman | 635 | Andrew Simpson, | Robert P. Harding, Assignee of R. K. Boyd. | Monlough, |
| | 636 | William Stevenson, | do. | do. |
| | 637 | Do. | do. | do. |
| | 638 | John Crawford, | do. | do. |
| | 639 | Roger Clarke, | do. | do. |
| | 640 | Do. | do. | do. |
| | 641 | Matthew Carlisle, | do. | do. |
| | 642 | John Thompson, | do. | do. |
| | 643 | James Scott, | do. | do. |
| | 644 | Samuel Ferguson, | Captain William Hearn, | Toughmore, |
| | 645 | James Ferguson, | do. | do. |
| | 646 | Hugh McVeagh, | J. G. Price, | Drumnaconnell, West, |
| | 647 | Andrew S. Oswald, | do. | do. |
| | 648 | Thomas Gillespie, | do. | Ballyanglterry, |
| | 649 | Hugh McVey, | do. | Linduigie, |
| | 650 | John McKee, | do. | Lisdoonan, |
| | 651 | Do. | do. | do. |
| | 652 | Samuel Strain, | do. | Killymore, |
| | 653 | David Campbell, | Robert N. Batt, | Ballyvaughlis, |
| | | | | Total, |

COUNTY OF

DOWN—*continued.*

| Extent of Holding. | Poor Law Valuation. | Former Rent. | Judicial Rent. | Observations. | Value of Tenancy. |
|---|---|---|---|---|---|
| A. R. P. | £ s. d. | £ s. d. | £ s. d. | | £ s. d. |
| 5 3 10 | 8 5 0 | 11 0 0 | 7 13 0 | | |
| 1 0 0 | 5 5 0 | 5 0 0 | 5 0 0 | | |
| 9 0 14 | 8 12 0 | 9 18 0 | 7 12 0 | | |
| 3 1 20 | unascertained, | 5 7 0 | 5 0 0 | | |
| 3 3 23 | do. | 6 19 0 | 5 15 0 | | |
| 4 1 0 | 5 5 0 | 7 17 10 | 5 0 0 | | |
| 5 2 30 | 7 5 0 | 10 16 2 | 7 17 0 | | |
| 3 0 0 | 6 0 0 | 6 16 2 | 5 13 0 | | |
| 13 3 25 | 11 15 0 | 15 0 0 | 11 15 0 | | |
| 15 3 20 | unascertained, | 16 18 0 | 15 15 0 | | |
| 1 2 25 | 1 0 0 | 5 10 0 | 3 3 0 | | |
| 29 3 21 | 21 10 0 | 16 0 0 | 15 6 0 | | |
| 5 2 20 | 1 10 0 | 5 10 0 | 5 10 0 | | |
| 5 1 15 | 2 5 0 | 5 0 2 | 5 13 0 | | |
| 5 3 17 | 5 0 0 | 5 16 0 | 7 10 0 | | |
| 5 1 23 | 0 10 0 | 10 5 0 | 7 5 0 | | |
| 7 0 50 | unascertained, | 5 6 3 | 5 5 0 | | |
| 10 2 3 | 11 0 0 | 9 13 5 | 5 15 0 | | |
| 15 5 5 | 19 10 0 | 16 10 6 | 15 0 0 | | |
| 31 3 23 | 50 10 0 | 50 12 13 | 55 15 0 | | |
| 55 0 0 | 71 15 0 | 75 0 0 | 51 0 0 | | |
| 450 0 33 | 355 10 0 | 458 16 5 | 552 15 0 | | |

} LONDONDERRY.

| Name of Assistant Commissioners by whom Cases were decided. | No. | Name of Tenant. | Name of Lan |
|---|---|---|---|
| HEAD COMMISSION. | 103 | James Armstrong, ... | Robert P. Ellis, |
|  | 104 | Alice McDonald, Rep. of Hugh McDonald. | Daniel M. Ross |

## MONAGHAN.

| Tenant of Holding. Acres. | Poor Law Valuation. £ s. d. | Former Rent. £ s. d. | Judicial Rent. £ s. d. | |
|---|---|---|---|---|
| A. R. P. | £ s. d. | £ s. d. | £ s. d. | |
| 63 1 6 | 52 6 0 | 58 0 0 | 50 0 0 | The |
| 4 1 25 | 4 0 0 | 7 3 6 | 6 6 0 | |
| 75 3 25 | 87 0 0 | 66 3 6 | 54 0 0 | |

## TYRONE

| | | | | |
|---|---|---|---|---|
| 10 1 25 | 6 10 0 | 7 10 0 | 8 10 0 | Ten |
| 68 3 23 | 63 15 0 | 33 5 0 | 25 0 0 | |
| 10 1 0 | — | 1 16 3 | 1 10 0 | |
| 18 0 7 | 10 15 0 | 10 15 0 | 6 13 0 | |
| | | | | |
| 43 1 4 | 40 15 0 | 33 15 6 | 30 0 6 | |
| 27 1 20 | 26 5 0 | 34 13 3 | 23 0 0 | |
| 34 1 11 | 15 10 0 | 17 15 6 | 14 0 0 | |
| 40 3 4 | 38 5 0 | 41 6 1 | 67 6 0 | |
| 64 0 25 | 33 15 0 | 26 1 9½ | 24 1 9½ | |
| 26 0 23 | 28 0 0 | 30 19 5 | 20 10 5 | |
| 90 3 30 | 23 0 0 | 23 6 6 | 10 0 0 | |
| 49 3 8 | 81 10 0 | 38 6 1 | 23 15 0 | |
| 45 0 20 | 38 5 0 | 31 0 0 | 28 3 0 | By |

# PROVINCE OF

## COUNTY OF

| Name of Assistant Commissioners by whom Cases were decided. | No. | Name of Tenant. | Name of Landlord. | Townland. |
|---|---|---|---|---|
| HEAD COMMISSION. | 385 | James Dwyer, | Rev. William Murl. | Rashenpish. |
| | 386 | Arthur Murphy, | Eugene Connolly, | Kilmurry, |
| | 387 | James Doyle, | do | Crean, |
| Assistant Commissioners— | 388 | Michael Summers, | Patrick R. Norton, | Killenan, |
| R. R. Kane (Legal). W. O. Della Foss. J. Hawksworth. | 389 | Harry Burgess, | Arthur Kavanagh, contd. in name of Walter McM. Kavanagh. | Killaughterram, |
| | | | | Total. |

COUNTY OF

# LEINSTER.

## CARLOW.

| Extent of Forfeited Estates | Poor Law Valuation | Former Rent |
|---|---|---|
| A. R. P. | £ s. d. | £ s. d. |
| 6 1 1 | 31 30 0 | 5 0 0 |
| 63 0 15 | 36 10 0 | 41 0 0 |
| 130 0 6 | 65 0 0 | 112 16 5 |
| 60 1 39 | 30 8 0 | 33 0 0 |
| 64 3 6 | 16 0 0 | 80 0 8 |
| 432 3 31 | 196 6 0 | 272 6 1 |

## DUBLIN.

# IRISH LAND COMMISSION.

| Names of Assistant Commissioners by whom Cases were decided. | No. | Name of Tenant. | Name of Landlord. | Townland. |
|---|---|---|---|---|
| HEAD COMMISSION. | 281 | John Hardy. — | John La Touche ... | — Baheybeg. |
| | 382 | Henry Travers, — | do. ... | ... Haheombeak, ... |
| | | | | Total, ... |

| | | | | |
|---|---|---|---|---|
| HEAD COMMISSION. | 436 | Henry Mathews, — | Robert Tyndall, ... | Milltown, — |
| Assistant Commissioners:— L. DOYLE (Legal). J. M. CARROLL. E. O. PERY. | 437 | Sarah Growyn, ... | W. H. Growse. — | — Growsse, — |
| | | | | Total, ... |

| | | | | |
|---|---|---|---|---|
| Assistant Commissioners:— M. Y. CREAN (Legal). T. DAVIDSON. J. H. MILLER. | 306 | Daniel Kane, ... | Peter M. Fisher, ... | ... KDrumaklin, — |
| M. T. CREAN (Legal). J. RICH. W. J. GOODMAN. | 307 | Catharine Quinlan, ... | Mrs. Lucy Stanjewie, ... | ... Corradarrae, ... |
| | | | | Total, — |

## KILKENNY.

| | | | | |
|---|---|---|---|---|
| 46  3  33 | 41  10  0 | 50  0  0 | 80  0  0 | The rent in this case was fixed by consent of the parties at the sitting of the Court in Dublin. |
| 175  3  6 | 134  16  0 | 120  0  0 | 100  0  0 | By consent. |
| 222  6  0 | 176  5  0 | 170  0  0 | 130  0  0 | |

## COUNTY.

| | | | | |
|---|---|---|---|---|
| 94  3  0 | 67  16  0 | 50  0  0 | 50  0  0 | |
| 29  0  26 | unascertained, | 27  0  0 | 13  0  0 | By consent. |
| 123  3  26 | 67  16  0 | 77  0  0 | 63  0  0 | |

## LONGFORD.

| | | | | |
|---|---|---|---|---|
| 16  3  9 | } 40  0  0 | { 30  0  0 | 50  0  0 | These two holdings were consolidated and a fair rent fixed by consent of the parties at the sitting of the Court in Dublin. |
| 34  1  33 | | 40  0  0 | | |
| 19  3  67 | 13  0  0 | 11  0  0 | 10  0  0 | The rent in this case was fixed by consent of the parties at the sitting of the Court in Dublin. |
| 70  3  29 | 53  0  0 | 71  0  0 | 60  0  0 | |

| Venue at Antorea Cunningham by whom Case was decided. | No. | Name of Tenant. | Name of Landlord. | Townland. |
|---|---|---|---|---|
| Head Commission. | 223 | Mary Drew, ... | Henry G. Singleton, ... | Noll, |

| | No. | Name of Tenant. | Name of Landlord. | Townland. |
|---|---|---|---|---|
| Head Commission. | 604 | Bernard Dillon, ... | John Tisdall, ... | ... | Phoenixtown, ... |
| | 603 | John McEvany, ... | H. S. Blackwood, ... | Derringhiy, ... |
| Assistant Commissioners— | 606 | Thomas Harlin, ... | George C. Smyth, ... | Piercetown, ... |
| W. P. Bailey (Legal). P. Magaffin. | 607 | Mrs. Ellen Cahill, ... | do. ... | do. |
| | | | | Total, ... |

| | No. | Name of Tenant. | Name of Landlord. | Townland. |
|---|---|---|---|---|
| Assistant Commissioners— | 303 | Ellen Harford, | Lord Congleton, ... | Ross, |
| R. B. Kaye (Legal). W. S. Huff. B. Martin. | 304 | John C. Moore, | Mrs. Harriet Moore & anor., | Clonrahan, |
| | 305 | Jane S. Walpole, | Colonel William Kennis, ... | Clone and anr. |
| | 306 | John Galvin, | Adelaide Arps, ... | Clonoharrig |
| | 307 | Do. ... | Christopher Meredith, ... | do. |
| | 308 | Edward Cullen, | Mrs. Elizabeth M. Pim, ... | Maher, |
| | 309 | Robert Empey, | W. L. Woodroofe, ... | Loughakon |
| | 310 | George Neale, | Captain Henry R. Despard and another, Trustees of Richard Despard, deceased. | Cashrode and anr. |
| | 311 | Thomas Cooper, | do. ... | do. |

| Law Valuation | Former Rent | Judicial Rent | Observations | Value of Tenancy |
|---|---|---|---|---|
| £ s. d. | £ s. d. | £ s. d. | | £ s. d. |
| 15 0 0 | 61 0 0 | 38 0 0 | The rent in this case was fixed by consent of the parties at the sitting of the Court in Dublin. | |

| | | | | |
|---|---|---|---|---|
| 62 10 0 | 98 0 0 | 78 0 0 | The rent in this case was fixed by consent of the parties at the sitting of the Court in Dublin, do. | |
| 01 0 0 | 67 10 0 | 54 0 0 | | |
| 159 0 0 | 160 0 0 | 179 0 0 | | |
| 48 0 0 | 60 0 0 | 61 15 0 | | |
| 349 10 0 | 185 10 0 | 319 15 0 | | |

| | | | | |
|---|---|---|---|---|
| 86 0 0 | 135 13 10 | 118 0 0 | Rent changed in 1879 £ s. d. from . . . 139 1 6 1887 100 1 2 | |
| 100 0 0 | 164 19 4 | 136 0 0 | | |
| 168 0 0 | 300 0 0 | 180 0 0 | | |
| 9 10 0 | 6 0 0 | 3 10 0 | | |
| 9 0 0 | 6 10 0 | 3 5 0 | | |
| 60 5 0 | 108 17 9 | 63 0 0 | | |
| 111 8 0 | 164 4 4 | 113 0 0 | | |
| 33 10 0 | 60 0 0 | 33 0 0 | | |
| 73 1 0 | 99 3 6 | 68 0 0 | | |
| 73 16 0 | 75 0 0 | 75 0 0 | | |
| 48 5 0 | 90 0 0 | 63 0 0 | | |

## IRISH LAND COMMISSION.

| Name of Assistant Commissioner by whom Case was decided. | No. | Name of Tenant. | Name of Landlord. |
|---|---|---|---|

| das | Former Rent. | | | Judicial Rent. | | | Observations. | Value of Tenancy |
|---|---|---|---|---|---|---|---|---|
| *l.* | *£* | *s.* | *d.* | *£* | *s.* | *d.* | | *£ s. d.* |
| 0 | 131 | 13 | 0½ | 96 | 10 | 0 | The rent in this case was fixed by consent of the parties at the sitting of the Court in Dublin. &c. | |
| 0 | 160 | 4 | 7 | 135 | 0 | 0 | | |
| 0 | 282 | 0 | 1½ | 231 | 10 | 0 | | |

| 0 | 7 | 13 | 4 | 6 | 0 | 0 | By consent. | |
|---|---|---|---|---|---|---|---|---|

| 0 | 14 | 0 | 0 | 19 | 0 | 0 | The rent in this case was fixed by consent of the parties at the sitting of the Court in Dublin. | |
|---|---|---|---|---|---|---|---|---|
| 0 | 108 | 0 | 0 | 61 | 0 | 0 | | |
| ½ | 30 | 0 | 0 | 15 | 0 | 0 | | |
| 0 | 43 | 10 | 0 | 32 | 0 | 0 | | |
| ½ | 32 | 0 | 0 | 16 | 0 | 0 | | |
| 0 | 916 | 10 | 0 | 155 | 0 | 0 | | |

# IRISH LAND COMMISSION.

# PROVINCE OF

## COUNTY OF

| Board of Assistant Commissioners by whom Case was decided. | No. | Name of Tenant. | Name of Landlord. | Townland. |
|---|---|---|---|---|
| Assistant Commissioners— | | | | |
| D. Tobery (Legal). R. Johnson. G. Vanderbilt. | 334 | Denis McGloin, | John Meehan, assied. in estate of Mary T. Meehan and ano. | Carrickmore, |
| | 335 | Carson McGloin, | do. | do. |
| | 336 | Owen Buddy, | do. | Drumashel, |
| | 337 | Terence McGloin, | do. | do. |
| | 338 | James McGowan, | do. | Drummore, |
| | 339 | Patrick McNulty. | do. | Meenmongangole, |
| M. T. Cosar (Legal). W. J. Gorman. J. Reid. | 340 | Joseph Nevill, | J. O. Lawder and another, | Aughamgala, |
| | 341 | Francis Ward, senior, | William C. B. Barhven, | Mucklaban, |
| | 342 | Richard Poston, | William R. Le Touche, | Dromlargan, |
| | 343 | Jane McDermott, | Lord Southwell, | Killanaghera, |
| | 344 | George Beatty, | Joseph Kean, | Dromalawlot, |
| | 345 | Thomas Barry, | do. | Dromkeelanmore, |
| | 346 | Andrew Byrne, | Earl of Albemarle, | Aughranmeldan, |
| | 347 | James Glasy, | do. | do. |
| | 348 | John Rutledge, | James R. Poyton, | Carrick, |
| | 349 | Michael Tighe, | do. | Carkery Poyton, |
| | 350 | Bridget Hanley, | do. | Carrick, |

# CONNAUGHT·

## LEITRIM.

| Extent of Holding. Statute. | Poor Law Valuation. | Former Rent. | Judicial Rent. | Observations. | Value of Tenancy. |
|---|---|---|---|---|---|
| A. R. P. | £ s. d. | £ s. d. | £ s. d. | | £ s. d. |
| 8 2 16 | 3 10 0 | 6 10 0 | 3 15 0 | By consent. | |
| 9 3 16 | 2 10 0 | 5 10 0 | 3 15 0 | do. | |
| 13 3 6 | 5 5 0 | 6 15 0 | 4 17 5 | do. | |
| 8 1 10 | 1 0 0 | 1 5 0 | 1 0 0 | do. | |
| 15 0 15 | 7 10 0 | 11 5 4 | 7 10 0 | do. | |
| 29 1 1 | 7 10 0 | 11 13 5 | 6 17 0 | do. | |
| | | | | | |
| 25 1 34 | 13 10 0 | 13 1 5 | 10 10 0 | | |
| 31 0 20 | 9 15 0 | 15 10 0 | 8 7 5 | | |
| 45 0 37 | 16 15 0 | 19 0 0 | 15 10 0 | | |
| 144 4 15 | 71 5 0 | 75 17 5 | 44 0 0 | | |
| 15 0 3 | 9 0 0 | 7 5 3 | 6 0 0 | | |
| 11 1 14 | 5 5 0 | 4 10 10½ | 4 5 0 | | |
| 16 1 42 | 6 9 0 | 7 0 0 | 6 6 0 | | |
| 23 2 14 | 7 10 0 | 10 0 0 | 7 11 0 | | |
| 34 0 6 | 16 6 0 | 20 0 0 | 14 10 0 | | |
| 51 0 35 | 23 8 0 | 25 0 0 | 20 0 0 | | |
| 23 1 30 | 16 10 0 | 18 0 0 | 15 3 0 | | |
| 649 2 3 | 215 6 0 | 260 15 1½ | 153 19 0 | | |

## ROSCOMMON.

| Extent of Holding. Statute. | Poor Law Valuation. | Former Rent. | Judicial Rent. | Observations. | Value of Tenancy. |
|---|---|---|---|---|---|
| 215 1 29 | 148 0 0 | 139 16 3 | 110 0 0 | The rent in this case was fixed by consent of the parties at the sitting of the Court in Dublin. | |
| 301 3 53 | 156 10 0 | 203 5 4 | 180 0 0 | | |
| 517 1 82 | 304 10 0 | 343 5 7 | 290 0 0 | | |

# IRISH LAND COMMISSION

## PROVINCE OF

### COUNTY OF

| Names of Assistant Commissioners by whom Cases were decided. | No. | Name of Tenant. | Name of Landlord. | Townland. |
|---|---|---|---|---|
| Assistant Commissioners :— | | | | |
| J. S. GREEN, q.c. (Legal). <br> J. MARTIN. <br> J. J. CRITT. | 937 | John Kelly and another, | Lothla G. L. Foster, ... | Knockalaghnaw, North and South. |
| | 938 | Thomas Murphy, — | Richard Griffith, ... | Magheramorne |

# MUNSTER.

## CLARE.

| Extent of Holding Statute. | Poor Law Valuation. | Former Rent | Judicial Rent. | Observations. | Value of Tenancy. |
|---|---|---|---|---|---|
| A. R. P. | £ s. d. | £ s. d. | £ s. d. | | £ s. d. |
| 862 9 33 | 79 0 0 | 103 0 0 | 80 0 0 | By consent. | |
| 112 0 0 | 15 10 0 | 23 13 10 | 17 0 0 | do. | |
| 479 9 33 | 94 10 0 | 127 13 10 | 97 3 0 | | |

## CORK.

| | | | | | |
|---|---|---|---|---|---|
| 63 0 0 | 19 0 0 | 34 0 0 | 25 10 0 | The rent in this case was fixed by consent of the parties at the sitting of the Court in Dublin. | |
| 8 0 81 | 11 0 0 | 33 0 0 | 16 10 0 | do. | |
| 50 3 10 | 15 13 0 | 20 0 0 | 15 10 0 | do. | |
| 20 3 3 | 14 18 0 | 30 15 0 | 21 0 0 | do. | |
| 34 0 30 | 17 16 0 | 23 0 0 | 17 0 0 | do. | |
| 69 2 34 | 33 0 0 | 48 17 4 | 40 0 0 | do. | |
| 163 1 6 | 108 10 0 | 175 15 1 | 133 10 0 | | |

## KERRY.

# IRISH LAND COMMISSION.

| Name of Assistant Commissioners by whom Cases were decided | No. | Name of Tenant. | Name of Landlord. | Townland. |
|---|---|---|---|---|
| Assistant Commissioners— | | | | |
| J. E. Green, Q.C. (Legal). J. Hammond. J. J. O'Halloran. | 1358 | John Devere, | Mrs. D. Massy, | Loughborough, |
| | 1359 | Michael O'Neill, | John P. White, | Ballyhealy, |
| | 1360 | Robert Harding, | Captain A. L. Sadlier, | Ardcummin, |
| | 1361 | John Sampson, | William Bentnell, | Kilgrane, |
| | 1362 | Richard Devere, | Charles W. Smith, | Oulimes, North, |
| | 1363 | John Fitzgerald, | do. | do. |
| | 1364 | James Reardon, | do. | do. |
| | 1365 | John Berke, | do. | do. |
| | 1366 | John Kaene, | do. | Oulimes, Middle, |
| | 1367 | Do. | do. | Oulimes, South, |
| | 1368 | Margaret McGrath, | do. | do. |
| | 1369 | Michael Tierney, | S. Morgan, M.D. | E.Glass, |
| | 1370 | Catherine Quish and another, | do. | do. |
| | 1371 | Thomas Carey, Trustee of P. Carey, | Nathaniel Buckley, | Knockmannon, |
| | 1372 | Lawrence D. Keane, | do. | Coolattin, |
| | 1373 | William Condon, | do. | Knockgourne, |
| | 1374 | William O'Brien, | Robert T. Webber, | Coolboy, |
| | 1375 | Edward Fitzgibbon, | do. | do. |
| | 1376 | Catherine Murray, Lict. Admix. of Edmund Murray. | do. | do. |
| | 1377 | Thomas Intrumten, | do. | Glenmorran, |
| | 1378 | Catherine Gallaghan, | do. | do. |
| | 1379 | Patrick Power, | do. | do. |
| | 1380 | Bridget Deasroy, | do. | S.Oglass, |
| | | | | Total. |

| Head Commissioners. | 1601 | Denis Keough, | Michael J. Hartigan, | Garryholin, |
|---|---|---|---|---|
| | 1602 | Terence O'Brien, | Darbre J. C. MacEgan and others. | Ballyvonglane, |
| | 1603 | Patrick Gannon, | Henry Langley, | Oualane, |

# LIMERICK—*continued.*

| Extent of Holding. | Poor Law Valuation. | Former Rent. | Judicial Rent. | Observations. | Value of Tenancy. |
|---|---|---|---|---|---|
| A. R. P. | £ s. d. | £ s. d. | £ s. d. | | £ s. d. |
| 93 2 37 | 18 15 0 | 90 1 2 | 28 0 0 | | |
| 73 0 33 | 63 0 0 | 108 0 0 | 85 10 0 | | |
| 85 1 33 | 27 0 0 | 65 7 6 | 35 15 0 | | |
| 7 3 8 | 6 0 0 | 7 6 0 | 6 15 0 | | |
| 27 0 5 | 10 0 0 | 24 4 8 | 19 10 0 | | |
| 13 0 23 | 5 10 0 | 13 11 3 | 8 8 0 | | |
| 34 4 14 | 16 15 0 | 48 9 6 | 24 0 6 | | |
| 42 3 34 | 35 15 0 | 96 15 0 | 60 0 6 | | |
| 16 0 5 | 7 10 0 | 17 6 6 | 10 6 0 | | |
| 22 0 0 | 13 0 0 | 33 2 8 | 16 15 0 | | |
| 19 1 30 | 6 15 0 | 15 15 0 | 7 0 0 | | |
| 15 4 60 | 13 5 0 | 19 16 6 | 15 0 0 | | |
| 30 1 0 | 20 5 0 | 28 6 0 | 30 0 0 | | |
| 23 3 34 | 14 0 0 | 22 0 0 | 20 0 0 | | |
| 11 2 35 | 9 15 0 | 6 5 3 | 8 5 0 | | |
| 28 1 30 | 21 0 0 | 34 10 0 | 24 0 0 | | |
| 42 3 15 | 10 2 0 | 14 0 0 | 10 10 0 | | |
| 14 2 33 | 7 10 0 | 9 13 0 | 8 0 0 | | |
| 5 1 24 | 3 15 0 | 3 5 0 | 1 13 0 | | |
| 87 1 3 | 8 5 0 | 11 0 0 | 8 0 0 | | |
| 44 3 13 | 11 0 6 | 14 0 0 | 19 0 0 | | |
| 39 1 19 | 10 0 9 | 10 16 0 | 8 10 0 | | |
| 16 3 51 | 8 15 0 | 8 10 0 | 5 5 0 | | |
| 1,010 2 28 | 613 5 0 | 845 18 7 | 611 9 8 | | |

TIPPERARY.

# IRISH LAND COMMISSION.

COUNTY OF

| Names of Assistant Commissioners by whom Cases were decided. | No. | Name of Tenant | Name of Landlord | Townland. |
|---|---|---|---|---|
| Assistant Commissioners—<br>J. A. Estes (Legal).<br>B. G. Peat.<br>F. M. Campbell. | 1004 | Edmund Butler, ... | Richard Hughes, ... | Ballyradise, — |
| | 1005 | John Halloran, ... | William A. Biall, ... | Nicholstown, — |
| | 1006 | Thomas O'Brien, ... | Anne Going and another, ... | Cappauagerrata, |
| | 1007 | Leonard Hill, ... | Averina M. Reade, ... | Bawnarvone, Lee. |
| | 1008 | James Carroll, ... | John Vaughan, ... | Flanane, — |
| | 1009 | John Vaughan, ... | Rev. W. R. Bryan, ... | Ballyrenters, — |
| | 1010 | William Ryan, ... | Richard H. Hughes and anor., | Ballyradise, — |
| | 1011 | Edmund Butler, Exor. of James Hackett. | Rev. R. D. Wright, cestui in cases of Miss S. E. Wright. | Mullinooly. |
| | 1012 | John W. Hughes, ... | Captain John Rodes, ... | Garramcnch, — |
| | 1013 | Arthur Bryan, — | William A. Going and anor., minors, by Arabella Going, their Guardian. | do. — |
| | 1014 | Anastatia Comerford, ... | Mrs. E. J. Guinness, ... | Clashbeg and another |
| | 1015 | Bridget Kickham and another. | William H. White, M.D. ... | Ballydwyer, |
| | 1016 | Thomas Marnell, ... | John Vaughan, ... | Flanane, — |
| | 1017 | Mathew Shortal, ... | Philip Cormack and another, | Mobehler, — |
| | 1018 | Patrick Carroll, ... | do. ... ... | do. — |
| | 1019 | Patrick Brophy, ... | do. ... ... | do. — |
| | 1020 | Thomas Hoynes, ... | do. ... ... | do. — |
| | 1021 | Michael Davey, ... | do. ... ... | do. — |
| | 1022 | Martin Byrne, ... | do. ... ... | do. — |
| | 1023 | John Rafter, ... | do. ... ... | do. — |
| | 1024 | Patrick Crowley, partd. in name of R. Crowley. | Dean W. G. Graves, ... | Ballinakissah, — |
| | 1025 | James Henry, ... | do. ... ... | do. — |
| | 1026 | William Curry, ... | William U. Townsend, partd. by Mary A. Townsend. | Ballinaggart, — |
| | 1027 | Philip Kennedy, ... | do. ... ... | do. — |
| | 1028 | William Cormcon, ... | John P. Hare, ... ... | Ballonghboy, — |
| | 1029 | Johanna Marnell, ... | do. ... ... | do. — |
| | 1030 | Patrick Flanane, ... | do. ... ... | do. — |
| | 1031 | Denis Flanane, ... | do. ... ... | do. — |
| | 1032 | Maurice Cronin, ... | do. ... ... | Ballingarry, — |
| | 1033 | Denis Flanane, ... | do. ... ... | Ballonghboy, — |
| | 1034 | Hugh Bryan, — | do, ... ... | Ballingarry, Upr. |
| | 1035 | Thomas O'Donnell, ... | do. ... ... | do. — |
| | 1036 | Do. — ... | do. ... ... | do. — |
| | 1037 | Bridget Crahn, ... | do. ... ... | Ballonghboy, — |

| Extent of Holding. Statute. | Poor Law Valuation. | Former Rent. | Judicial Rent. | Observations. | Value of Tenancy. |
|---|---|---|---|---|---|
| A. R. P. | £ s. d. | £ s. d. | £ s. d. | | £ s. d. |
| 77 1 29 | 45 10 0 | 50 0 0 | 12 0 0 | | |
| 125 3 30 | 113 5 0 | 101 11 6 | 52 7 0 | By consent. | |
| 0 0 53 | 5 10 0 | 7 2 2 | 7 2 3 | | |
| 11 1 14 | 6 13 0 | 7 0 0 | 5 3 0 | | |
| 12 1 90 | 5 10 0 | 7 0 0 | 6 0 0 | | |
| 61 0 63 | 49 15 0 | 48 0 0 | 46 0 0 | | |
| 54 0 27 | 46 13 0 | 54 0 0 | 38 10 0 | | |
| 60 2 34 | uncertain land, | 46 11 0 | 39 17 8 | | |
| 105 1 0 | 12 0 0 | 100 0 0 | 87 0 0 | | |
| 147 0 4 | 104 0 0 | 178 10 0 | 181 0 0 | | |
| 69 3 13 | 83 10 0 | 65 9 0 | 65 0 0 | | |
| 10 3 53 | uncertain land, | 77 11 4 | 14 10 0 | | |
| 131 5 34 | 65 5 0 | 61 0 0 | 63 0 0 | | |
| 0 0 18 | 8 5 0 | 6 0 0 | 4 13 0 | | |
| 4 2 21 | 6 0 0 | 5 17 5 | 3 12 0 | | |
| 10 3 26 | 9 0 0 | 8 16 1 | 6 10 0 | | |
| 9 1 1 | 34 15 0 | 23 10 0 | 21 0 0 | | |
| 23 0 8 | 63 15 0 | 40 6 3 | 46 0 0 | | |
| 11 3 6 | 10 6 0 | 12 3 10 | 5 10 0 | | |
| 49 0 33 | 34 10 0 | 45 13 0 | 30 0 0 | | |
| 51 3 3 | 40 0 0 | 44 8 8 | 36 0 0 | | |
| 97 2 13 | 79 0 0 | 134 0 0 | 110 0 0 | | |
| 123 0 0 | 34 14 0 | 56 0 0 | 5 0 0 | | |
| 73 1 39 | 37 10 0 | 43 0 0 | 43 0 0 | | |
| 28 0 33 | 14 0 0 | 16 2 1 | 13 10 0 | | |
| 77 3 43 | 16 0 0 | 18 6 11 | 13 10 0 | | |
| 130 2 11 | 76 0 0 | 87 19 7 | 70 0 0 | | |
| 57 0 21 | 87 0 0 | 37 10 3 | 37 10 0 | | |
| 9 1 23 | 3 14 0 | 5 17 3 | 3 0 0 | | |
| 18 0 37 | 8 0 0 | 11 6 0 | 9 10 0 | | |
| 60 0 10 | 50 10 0 | 47 16 1½ | 13 0 0 | | |
| 54 1 7 | 34 5 0 | 30 15 6 | 20 10 4 | | |
| 81 2 13 | 16 14 0 | 19 16 5 | 15 0 0 | | |
| 54 6 23 | 31 10 0 | 50 7 4 | 44 0 0 | | |

| Names of Assistant Commissioners by whom Cases were decided. | No. | Name of Tenant. | Name of Landlord. | Townland. |
|---|---|---|---|---|
| Assistant Commissioners :— | | | | |
| J. H. Ross (Legal). | 1038 | William Molloy, contd. in name of Mary Molloy. | John F Hire, — | Balloughboy, — |
| R. G. Prior | 1039 | William Carrucan, — | do. | do. |
| P. M. Carroll | 1040 | Thomas Murphy, | do. | do. |
| | 1041 | Michael Croke, | do. | do. |
| | 1042 | Edmond Croke, contd. in name of James Croke. | do. | Ballaughreel, — |
| | 1043 | James McGrath, | do. | Ballingarry, Lr. |
| | 1044 | Thomas O'Donnell, | do. | Ballingarry, Up. |
| | 1045 | Patrick Maher, — | Lord Longford and anor., Trustees of Thomas Ponsonby, a minor. | Shragarry and another. |
| | 1046 | Ellen Maher, | do. | do. |
| | 1047 | Oliver Fitzgerald, | do. | Williard, |
| | 1048 | Thomas Hinkey, a minor, by Hugh Hinkey, his Guardian. | do. | Craigunakenka, |
| | 1049 | Michael Power, | do. | Craigunakenka and another. |
| | 1050 | Ellen Brien, — | do. | Shanagarry. |
| | 1051 | Michael Teehan, | do. | Williard, |
| | 1052 | Michael Power, contd. in name of Honora Power. | do. | Shanagarry. |
| | 1053 | Mary Magrath, | Mary G. Purse, — | Farmingshog |
| | 1054 | Patrick Carmack, | do. | do. |
| | 1055 | John Ouahlley, — | A. H. Knox, | Islands and anor. |
| | 1056 | Edward Kickham, | Capt. W. R. Pallisor, | Terrant, |
| | 1057 | Thomas O'Brien, | do. | do. |
| | 1058 | Cornelius Burke, | Col. F. E. R. Tighe, | Kilbahoon, |
| | 1059 | Samuel Wilson, contd. in name of James Wilson, his Assignee. | G. Power Lalor, — | Kilnamo, |
| | 1060 | Thomas O'Brien and anor., Trustees of Thos. O'Brien. | Robert Barfield and others. | Lawlerstown, |
| | 1061 | John Keeffe, — | R. F. Croughan, | Ballivocker, |
| | 1062 | Denis Aherne, | John Hall, — | Ballyradish and another. |
| | | | | Total, — |

| Extent of Holding. Quantity. | Poor Law Valuation. | Former Rent. | Judicial Rent. | Observations. | Value of Tenancy. |
|---|---|---|---|---|---|
| a. r. p. | £ s. d. | £ s. d. | £ s. d. | | £ s. d. |
| 40 2 29 | 29 5 6 | 53 15 5 | 31 0 0 | | |
| 1 0 39 | 1 15 0 | 2 5 11 | 3 5 11 | | |
| 20 2 8 | 8 15 0 | 11 0 1 | 10 0 0 | | |
| 68 2 22 | 85 10 0 | 80 8 9 | 37 0 0 | | |
| 31 1 37 | 16 15 0 | 16 4 5 | 16 10 9 | | |
| 9 1 10 | 6 0 0 | 8 5 4 | 7 0 0 | | |
| 6 0 21 | 7 5 0 | 11 6 11 | 7 0 0 | | |
| 43 0 15 | 30 5 0 | 12 9 6 | 27 10 0 | | |
| 55 2 3 | 33 10 0 | 38 0 0 | 19 10 0 | | |
| 134 1 7 | 101 5 0 | 116 8 10 | 98 0 0 | | |
| 113 0 17 | 81 10 0 | 100 0 0 | 79 0 0 | | |
| 237 0 0 | 176 5 0 | 185 0 0 | 197 10 8 | | |
| 28 2 27 | 96 0 0 | 38 5 0 | 28 0 0 | | |
| 85 3 36 | 18 5 0 | 18 3 10 | 16 5 0 | | |
| 91 0 35 | 15 10 0 | 16 17 8 | 13 15 0 | | |
| 85 1 26 | 16 10 0 | 11 7 0 | 13 0 0 | | |
| 89 3 15 | 17 0 0 | 13 15 11 | 11 10 9 | | |
| 538 1 10 | 303 15 0 | 604 10 0 | 236 0 0 | | |
| 47 0 0 | 28 0 0 | 84 0 0 | 37 15 0 | | |
| 65 2 30 | 68 15 0 | 49 0 0 | 38 10 0 | | |
| 43 3 28 | 25 15 0 | 50 0 0 | 27 0 0 | | |
| 39 0 53 | 34 0 0 | 21 0 0 | 18 0 0 | | |
| 63 0 18 | 74 10 0 | 89 15 10 | 71 10 0 | | |
| 47 3 16 | *unoccupied.* | 57 10 0 | 50 0 0 | | |
| 68 0 30 | 63 10 0 | 180 0 0 | 57 0 0 | | |
| 3,397 3 19 | 2,558 5 0 | 3,451 2 5½ | 2,696 8 3 | | |

WATERFORD.

# CIVIL BILL

## PROVINCE OF

### COUNTY OF

| No. | Name of Tenant. | Name of Landlord. | Townland. |
|---|---|---|---|
| 15 | Thomas Graham, | — A. H. Irvine, ... | Edenagor — |
| 16 | Robert Britton, ... | Major Arthur J. Armstrong, | Drumacommah, — |
| | | | Total, — |

## PROVINCE OF

### COUNTY OF

| No. | Name of Tenant. | Name of Landlord. | Townland. |
|---|---|---|---|
| 94 | James A. Smith, | — Thomas O. Wren, | Keenaghan — |
| 95 | Patrick Lowe, | — Reps. of Ellen Patrick, | Ballin, — |
| 96 | Judith Dempsey, | — do. | do. — |
| 97 | John Flynn | — do. | Ballin and end, — |
| 98 | Thomas Kennedy, | ... Earl of Essex, — | Blackfriary, — |
| 99 | Lawrence Daly, | — Rep. of James Tyrrel, | Pebbletown, — |
| 100 | Peter May, | ... Henry Hodgins. ... | Kilmaboy, — |
| | | | Total, — |

### COUNTY OF

# COURTS.

## ULSTER.

### FERMANAGH.

| Tenants of Holding. Stat.A. | Poor Law Valuation | Former Rent. | Judicial Rent. | Observations. | Value of Tenantry. |
|---|---|---|---|---|---|
| A. R. P. | £ s. d. | £ s. d. | £ s. d. | | £ s. d. |
| 19 3 8 | 8 5 0 | 9 9 6 | 6 16 0 | | |
| 29 2 9 | 18 0 0 | 19 18 7 | 12 0 0 | | |
| 12 0 12 | 24 5 0 | 29 6 3 | 16 16 0 | | |

## LEINSTER.

### MEATH

| 373 0 21 | 189 10 0 | 170 10 9 | 158 0 0 | | |
|---|---|---|---|---|---|
| 48 3 63 | 39 0 0 | 44 6 1 | 37 0 0 | | |
| 88 2 29 | 19 10 0 | 24 17 0 | 20 0 8 | | |
| 39 4 53 | 39 15 0 | 33 16 0 | 26 15 0 | | |
| 117 3 6 | 271 0 0 | 300 13 0 | 215 0 0 | | |
| 47 0 23 | 60 0 0 | 44 0 0 | 53 0 0 | | |
| 16 3 16 | 70 0 0 | 21 0 0 | 14 10 0 | | |
| 631 1 39 | 688 15 0 | 764 3 10 | 641 5 0 | | |

### WICKLOW.

PROVINCE OF

COUNTY OF

| County Court Judge. | No. | Name of Tenant. | Name of Landlord. | Townland. |
|---|---|---|---|---|
| J. H. Bernard, Q.C. | 87 | William Browne, ... | Edmund A. Ryan, ... | Rossbrien, North |

PROVINCE OF

COUNTY OF

| County Court Judge. | No. | Name of Tenant. | Name of Landlord. | Townland. |
|---|---|---|---|---|
| J. F. Hawnden, Q.C. | 253 | John Turpin, ... | Rev. John W. Nolgin & ors., | Dawstown. — |
| | 254 | Michael Cronin, ... | do. ... ... | Knockaunatably. |
| | | | | Total, — |

COUNTY OF

# CONNAUGHT.

## MAYO.

| Extent of Holding Square. | Poor Law Valuation. | Former Rent. | Judicial Rent. | Observations. | Value of Tenancy. |
|---|---|---|---|---|---|
| A. R. P. | £ s. d. | £ s. d. | £ s. d. | | £ s. d. |
| 13 0 P | 8 0 0 | 12 0 0 | 8 10 0 | | |

# MUNSTER

## CORK.

Return Based upon the Reports of Valuers appointed by the Irish Land Commission on the Joint Application of Landlords and Tenants.

## COUNTY OF CORK.

| No. | Name of Tenant | Name of Landlord | Townland | Present or Existing Rent | Poor Law Valuation | Former Rent | Present Rent | Observations |
|---|---|---|---|---|---|---|---|---|
| | | | | £ s. d. | £ s. d. | £ s. d. | £ s. d. | |
| | | | | | | | | |
| | | | | | | | | |
| | | | | | | | | |
| | | | | | | | | |
| | | | | | | | | |
| | | | Total ... | | | | | |

www.ingramcontent.com/pod-product-compliance
Lightning Source LLC
Chambersburg PA
CBHW031454270326
41930CB00007B/1002